REVI

A moving story about a large Italian family fractured by loss and mental illness. Jerry writes from the heart about the transformative power of music, spirituality, love and community. This is about endurance, determination, and survival: to become whole and to love.
~Linda Joy Myers, PhD., author of *Becoming Whole: Writing Your Healing Story* and *Don't Call Me Mother*, Berkeley, CA

It is not so much courage as inner necessity that has required Jerry Smith to continue her role as family storyteller by bearing witness to the truly extra-ordinary story of her family and herself. It still is somethat mysterious how one child, not to mention several, can survive a truly heartrending childhood so well. We speak of "parentified children," and it's true, Jerry seemed forced into that role by circumstance. She could have chosen to "act out," but she did not.

Sometimes, though, a child enters the world with a special connection to Something Larger (call it what you will,) here represented by Jerry's connection with spirituality and by her deep connection with music.

The story is no "easy retreat to God," denying the role of human emotion. It is instead a story of a deep spirituality, present from birth, severely tested, but which supported Jerry allowing her safe passage through sometimes devastating emotional lows and highs of her life.

No doubt her remaining siblings would have a different story to tell, and one hopes they might do so. But this is Jerry's story.

It is my privilege to commend it to you.
~Karlyn Ward, PhD., Jungian Analyst, Mill Valley, CA

Jerry Smith has written a moving account of the power of the human spirit to transcend loss and difficulty, even when we are very young. *We Were Not Orphans* is an inspiring a testimonial to the strength of families to heal even the deepest of wounds.
~Rachel Naomi Remen MD, Author, *Kitchen Table Wisdom*

We Were Not
Orphans

Geraldine M. Smith

We Were Not
Orphans

Geraldine M. Smith

We Were Not Orphans

ACKNOWLEDGMENTS

*T*his book could not have been written without the encouragement and support of many people. My sister, Rosalie, was always available to remind me of details and incidents I had forgotten, until her untimely death. Almost all of my sisters and brothers would rather forget the troublesome times we each had at the orphanage and at home when our parents tried to prevent us from knowing of their inability to support and care for us.

Linda Joy Meyers patiently taught me how to write my story and without her this would never have seen print. Her book, *Becoming Whole: Writing Your Healing Story* was most helpful. Karlyn Ward, Marya Marthas, Joy and Eldon Ernst had gentle words of kindness which kept me writing. My childhood friend, Helen Schwartz Bell, read a small portion of my memoir and continued to encourage me throughout my struggle to write.

My sisters, Doris and Charlotte, and brothers, David, Ronald, Chase, and Vincent were gracious in allowing me to write our story from my experience even though there were times they were concerned that family secrets might hinder some of their friendships. My intention was to avoid hurting anyone. I trust my siblings will feel free to tell their own stories for we may have different experiences of the same events.

Rachel Naomi Remen's memoir, *Kitchen Table Wisdom*, first inspired me to recognize that healing can occur when one tells one's own difficult story. To Rachel I am very grateful. John Byng-Hall's discussion of parentified children was also most helpful in understanding my own role as one of those children "parentified."

Thanks to Mindy Toomey and Janet Carter who made suggestions beyond copy editing to assist me in creating a final draft. Linda and Robert Vaughn were generous in their time and patience that brought the document and old photos ready for publishing. Cathi Stevenson and Gwen Gades produced the cover design and layout which made me proud of their work.

My husband, Archie, lovingly and patiently assisted me when my computer skills were wanting and always had a word of wisdom and encouragement when I became discouraged because he believed my story needed to be told.

"Strong Women," my weight training class, will never know how much their encouragement meant to me as we faithfully performed the exercises to maintain our strong bones.

Thanks to you the reader for allowing me to share my story with you. May it inspire you to write your own memoir.

CHAPTER ONE

THE DEPARTURE

*M*y sisters and I watched from the front window of our house on Josephine Street as a black car pulled up in front and stopped. A woman wearing a dark coat and carrying a black handbag and black notebook got out and walked to our door.

I hoped this wasn't the social worker Daddy had said would come for us. She had gray hair, wore glasses but no lipstick, and had on old-fashioned shoes with thick heels. Her thin lips made her look stern. Maybe she was expecting to have a fight with Daddy. I knew he did not want us taken away from him.

Daddy bent his head as he answered the door. The lady came in and stood with her coat on, refusing his invitation to sit down. "Are the girls ready?" she said briskly. "They don't need to take anything with them. They'll be getting clothes and shoes at the orphanage."

It was nineteen forty-four and I was twelve years old and I had heard about this orphanage. I thought only children with no parents were orphans and couldn't understand how we could be taken to an orphanage when we had our Mom and Dad, but I was afraid to ask questions. My little sisters clustered around me and I tried to be strong.

Soon the lady ushered the four of us down the stairs. Daddy hung his head and followed. Why didn't he say anything? He was in his dirty work clothes, with cement still sticking to his khaki-colored shirt and pants. I looked up at him. He had always seemed so tall and strong. He had to be, for his work at Mondo Construction Company—paving streets, sidewalks, and driveways, digging ditches for sewer pipes, and laying bricks for foundations. I knew he was proud of his strength.

But now, I saw tears streaming down his ruddy, weather-beaten face. This was the first time any of us had seen him cry. He was still a handsome man, with black curly hair and a rugged face, but today his shoulders were hunched. Today he did not seem strong. He just looked sad, beaten down, and upset. Our family was being broken up because Mom had been taken to the state mental hospital, and there was nothing Dad could do to prevent it.

Charlotte was just three and Doris five. They began crying, too. I kept from sobbing by clenching my teeth and tightening my lips, as I still do as an adult. I needed to take care of my sisters, like I was used to doing. Rosalie aged ten, looked very frightened but she didn't cry until Daddy hugged and kissed her, stroking her curly auburn hair.

When he leaned down to hug and kiss Doris and gently tug her pigtails, she began wailing, "Daddy I want to stay home with you!" Charlotte picked up the refrain and cried louder, "Me too, Daddy." He picked up Charlotte and hugged her, stroking her kinky, light-brown hair.

"You gotta go with Jerry, Rosalie, and Doris to the orphanage," he told her quietly. "I'll come see you. You know you are my *'piccialidda,' my little girl.*"

Doris clung to one of his legs and Charlotte to the other, but Daddy released their grips, took their hands, and walked the four of us to the social worker's car. Charlotte was carrying the rag doll Mom had made for her. There had never been enough money to buy dolls or other toys, so this one was special.

The social worker said in a cold voice, "Okay, girls, climb in. It's time to go."

We crawled into the sedan one by one, Charlotte and Doris still crying as I helped them step up into the car. All four of us huddled together in the back seat. Rosalie was drying her tears on the hem of her dress, trying to act very grown up. My eyes were watering, too, but I fought back the tears. I was worried about Daddy being left alone. He came and stood next to the car, took his red handkerchief from his back pocket, and wiped his eyes. Then he leaned over and said "*Stata tenda.*" Take care. He was always saying that.

The social worker slammed our car door. We all jumped. Before she got into the driver's seat, Daddy asked, "You sure I visit my children? *Promesa,* they come home some Sundays?" When he was upset, he always mixed Italian in with his English.

The lady in black reassured him in a voice that sounded annoyed. "Yes, Mr. Messina, you can visit some evenings and every weekend, and you can even bring them home sometimes." He shook his head as if he wasn't sure he could trust her words.

As we drove away, I realized that none of the neighbors had come to say good-bye, though they were probably watching us from behind their living room curtains. I wondered if we would ever see any of them again.

Baby Fran, Josephine St. House
Syracuse, NY

CHAPTER TWO

THE ARRIVAL

The social worker looked straight ahead as she drove us away, ignoring the sniffles from the backseat. Silently, she took us through neighborhoods we had never seen before.

After a few minutes she said, "The Onondaga Orphans Home will be your new home. It is perched on one of the seven high hills that Syracuse is famous for—just like Rome. It is a long way from the Italian north side of Syracuse where you've been living. You'll be transferred to a new school."

There was nothing we could say and we remained quiet on the long ride up the hill past large houses with well-kept green lawns. I noticed how these homes contrasted with those on Josephine Street, where there were no lawns out front so we played in the street.

I began wondering about my music. The social worker had said not to pack anything, but maybe I should have tried to bring some of my recent piano pieces. I had just started practicing the Beethoven *Impassionata*. It was very difficult, but Mrs. Myrtle showed me how to take a section at a time when I began a new sonata, so that I would not get overwhelmed by trying to master the whole thing at once.

At my first glimpse of the orphans' home I was awed by its size. What seemed like a dozen large gray buildings were scattered around a huge area. A chain at the entrance was unlocked and pulled back for us to enter. As we drove through, the social worker said, "This gate is locked at night, so you will be safe."

Would they lock us in and never let us out? I decided I shouldn't let my sisters see how scared I was. I kept my feelings inside, and tightened my jaw the way I still do when I'm scared.

I noticed the street sign: Salt Springs Road. I remembered from my fourth grade history that Syracuse was noted since the time of the Onondaga Indians as the "Salt City" because of salt deposits on the shores of the lake. Daddy used to take us to the French Fort overlooking Onondaga Lake, and had told us stories about the Frenchmen who traded with the Indians at the Fort. We really enjoyed those outings. Would we ever see our Daddy, our brothers, our home or the French Fort again?

The social worker turned into the circular road separating the drab gray stucco buildings from the playground where the swings and slides were empty. The children must be at school, I reasoned. She called the buildings "cottages" but they did not look like the small and cozy cottages I'd read about in fairy tales. I counted nine imposing three-story buildings facing the playground and several smaller buildings, each one surrounded by green lawn.

The social worker read the names of the cottages as we slowly passed them. "This is Rose Bud, but that's not where you'll be living. It's where some of the staff of the orphanage live. The next three are for girls: Blue Bell, Blue Bird, and Marigold." The names sounded very pretty, despite the drab buildings. The girls' cottages were exactly alike. When we drove past Blue Bell I looked for blue bell flowers, but there were none in sight. There were no marigolds in front of Marigold Cottage either. We four girls were assigned to Blue Bird, but of course there were no blue birds singing in the trees. Pointing to the other side of the playground, the social worker told us the names of the boys' cottages: Tigris Patrol, Boy Scout, Hiawatha, and Rough Riders. Those buildings were partially hidden by tall, swaying elm trees. The scene seemed eerily quiet. The cottages looked so much alike that I began to worry we would get mixed up and go to the wrong one when we came home from school. For a long time, I had been a worrier. Now there were so many more things to worry about—getting lost in this huge place, how my younger siblings would be treated, how long we would be here. I remembered Daddy saying, "*Stata Tenda*" take care. He was alone now, with Mom in the hospital and all of us kids taken away.

As we pulled into the driveway next to Blue Bird cottage, my sisters and I clung tighter to each other. I kept touching and hugging them, whispering, "We'll be all right, we're still together." We did not speak about our brothers, who were not with us. I guess we were not really all together, but I didn't know what else to say to reassure my sisters and myself.

Rosalie took Doris's hand and I took Charlotte's and put my arm around her as we followed the social worker up the sidewalk to the front door of Blue Bird, our new home. Because we'd been told we would be getting clothes and shoes at the orphanage, we carried nothing, except for Charlotte who was still clinging to her dirty raggedy doll. Last year someone from our parents' church had given Charlotte a used tricycle, and though its wheels were bent, we all loved to watch her try to ride it. Those happy times seemed so far away now.

I whispered to Rosalie, "You'll need to count when you come home from school so you won't go to the wrong cottage." I wanted to put Rosalie at ease, seeing now a familiar frightened look in her eyes.

She said, "I can't see the signs over the front doors, they're so small."

"Don't worry, you can count!" I kidded.

She nodded, but didn't smile.

A stern, imposing woman, the matron of Blue Bird, met us at the door saying, "Call me Mother Swind."

She was very tall, and large-boned, with broad shoulders like a man. I thought I had never seen such a big woman. I was immediately afraid of her. I saw the fear in Doris and Charlotte's eyes, too, and put my arms around them.

With as much confidence as I could muster, I asked the social worker, "When will we see our brothers?"

"Soon," she said. "There were no vacancies in the boys' cottages, so they were taken to a foster home until there is room for them here. Probably they will be assigned to Hiawatha soon."

I wondered how long "soon" was but I was afraid to ask. I missed David and Ronnie already and worried about them. They were always getting into mischief. Although the boys were seven and eight, they looked so much alike that they enjoyed teasing people, asking them to guess their names, pretending they were identical twins. Ronnie was David's shadow following him everywhere. At home they were inseparable. I wondered whether Dad knew they were in a foster home. If he knew, why didn't he tell us girls? He usually told me everything.

Before leaving us, the social worker said, "You'll be fine here in Blue Bird with Mother Swind. Good-bye, then." We never saw her again.

Mrs. Swind did not take us through the cottage herself but assigned the task to one of the older girls, who had just returned from school. "This is Alicia. She'll show you around."

Alicia was about 15, tall, with long, curly honey-colored hair. She had a warm smile, and I liked her right away. She put us at ease saying, "First, I'll show you where you will be sleeping, follow me upstairs."

As we trooped across the shiny black linoleum floors Alicia told us all about the rules and expectations. "We all help to keep Blue Bird clean and polished. We have the reputation of having the cleanest cottage of all. Mother Swind will assign chores for each of you tomorrow. We all have chores to do and must do them every day except our birthdays, the only time we get a holiday."

There were four dorm rooms. One had eight white iron beds for the older girls and Rosalie and I were each assigned a bed and two dresser drawers in that room. Doris and Charlotte were assigned to the seven-bed dorm and given one dresser drawer each. "More beds are added at times," Alicia explained, "when we need to sleep more girls.

At home I had always shared a bed with Rosalie and sometimes all four of us girls would sleep in the same bed to keep each other warm. Having my own bed would be lonely and cold. If I awoke during the night it was comforting to hear my sisters breathing next to me. My stomach felt hollow as we proceeded down the hall. Alone in bed. One more thing to get used to.

Rosalie spoke my thoughts, "Can't we all sleep in the same room?"

Alicia shook her head, "No, all the other beds are taken."

The large bathroom had three toilets, two bathtubs and a shelf along one wall for toothbrushes, toothpaste, combs and other articles, and wall hooks for towels for each girl. A gigantic mirror covered one wall and a bank of windows on the opposite wall looked out over the back yard. The whole room was painted white and was clean, light, and airy. The trough-like sink in the center was about six feet long and had faucets on both sides so all 25 to 30 girls could get ready for school each morning.

We weren't used to such a well-equipped bathroom. Doris

moved closer to me and whispered, "Will we have our own towel and washcloth?" Hoping to offer a positive note I nodded yes, "Isn't that good?" But she just shrugged her shoulders.

Alicia showed us the small ironing room and pointed out a cubby hole for each of us where our underwear, play and school clothes, and Sunday outfits would be kept. She said we would be given three sets of new clothes for play, three for school, and three for Sunday. Clothes just for me? At home, I would trade off with Rosalie when one of us had run out of clean dresses for school so that we didn't have to wear the same thing the whole week. Seldom did we have new clothes, mostly hand-me-downs from relatives or friends from church. We thought it was the way everyone lived, with clothes from friends.

Rosalie asked in amazement, "You mean we can choose what we want to wear to school?"

Alicia smiled, "Yes, you can select whatever you want to wear as long as they are school clothes."

As we continued our tour, Alicia pointed to a door, "That's Mother Swind's bedroom; we are not allowed in there." Another door that led to a stairway to the third floor where the cook slept, was also off limits.

Next Alicia took us downstairs, where about fifteen young children were running around a large cement-floored room, some playing dodge ball. A large box of toys sat in one corner. The sun was streaming through large windows on three sides of the room. She called the room the playroom.

Alicia smiled at Charlotte and said, "Since you are too young to go to school you will be able to play in this room all day with four other little girls who don't go to school yet."

I hugged Charlotte, saying, "That will be fun, honey, won't it?" She nodded, but I couldn't get her to smile.

Alicia continued teaching us our new routine. "You all will be assigned a hook to hang your coats and jackets and a locker to store your boots in when you come in from outdoors. Most of the kids stay in the playroom after school, if it's bad weather." Then she mentioned, "We never enter Blue Bird through the front door, only through the playroom door." I finally spoke my worries out loud.

"We might have trouble picking out Blue Bird if we use the path to the playroom, since all the cottages look alike and the only sign is over the front door."

Alicia's smile reassured me that I might have at least one person here who understood. "All of us have gotten mixed up at least once and gone to the wrong cottage. They do look alike from the outside."

Some of the younger children were banging on an out-of-tune upright piano in the playroom. I felt a pang of fear that moving to the orphanage might be the end of my piano lessons. At home when I played, I would get lost in the music which helped me deal with confusion and worry. No one would interrupt or make demands of me when I was at the piano.

I loved playing for hours at a time. Would that change at Blue Bird where there was so much to get used to? I silently prayed that my music would help me cope with the intimidating Mrs. Swind and living with 26 other girls.

Alicia continued the tour, the huge rooms and stairways and halls became more and more confusing. It would be so easy to get lost.

The small laundry room had large slate tubs. Alicia said the laundry was done for all the cottages by the orphanage's own laundry in the basement of the Administration Building, but that sometimes the younger girls wet their beds and their sheets had to be washed out in these tubs.

She said, "We older girls have to help them."

I understood her meaning—I was one of the older girls who would be washing out sheets.

Alicia led us toward the kitchen. She said the older girls were assigned to wash and dry dishes and pots and pans in the two large sinks, and she pointed to the walk-in pantry where enormous cans of food were stored. Alicia told us that the cook always locks it when she wasn't in the kitchen, so kids don't steal cookies and crackers and take them to their beds.

I was surprised at the size of the huge cast-iron stove with its eight burners and two ovens. Rosalie commented, "Wow, what a big stove." We nodded in agreement. I had never seen a stove this large. There was no place for coal and a fire like the stove we had at home. The kitchen smelled so good, I thought something delicious must be baking in the oven. In the dining room, there were six round tables already set for supper.

"That table nearest the window is Mother Swind's table. We are not allowed to sit with her. We have assigned seats and probably you will sit with your little sister so you can help her." That was a relief. At three, Charlotte still needed me to take care of her.

The dining room windows looked out toward the front lawn and we could see the boys' cottages in the distance beyond the tall elm trees.

The largest room in the house was the living room situated on the opposite side of the dining room, with the front entrance and vestibule in between. The wooden mission-style furniture didn't look as if anyone ever sat on it. A window bench on each side of the brick fireplace with a window above the cushioned seat looked very inviting. I thought it would be a good place to read—my second favorite way to escape my worries. The classic painting, Blue Boy, hung on one wall and it seemed out of place to me in a girls' cottage until I discovered Blue Girl, the companion painting, on another wall. They seemed like such old-fashioned pictures.

The only picture we had in the living room at home was of a lone wolf howling on a snowy hill at night. It was one of Mom's favorites. I never understood why. To me, it had such a lonely feeling.

A brown rug partially covered the black linoleum floor and made the room seem more comfortable than any of the others. I gazed at the polished upright piano in one corner, longing to touch it, and to hear its tone. I stared at it while Alicia listed a number of rules:

1. No one is allowed to go into the living room unless they have visitors but there aren't many visitors. (The assumption being that we Messina girls wouldn't have visitors, either.)

2. No one is allowed to sit on the living room furniture in dungarees because Mrs. Swind says jeans will wear out the upholstery." Alicia whispered an aside, "That's only a rule in Blue Bird, the other matrons don't have that rule."

3. No one is allowed to talk in the study where we do our

homework. A large oak table with heavy oak chairs took up most of the room and a built-in book case lined one wall.

4. "No one is allowed in Mrs. Swind's bedroom."

"No one is allowed..." "No one is allowed..." There were more rules but she said we could wait until later to hear them. So many rules! Would I remember them, and how would I help my sisters remember them? There was so much more now to learn and worry about.

We were to register the next day at Charles Andrews School, just around the corner from the orphanage, a school with kindergarten through ninth grade. I had been going to a junior high school, while my sisters and brothers attended elementary school. I was pleased that now we'd all be in the same school.

Alicia told us that everyone in the orphanage used to wear uniforms to school, but now everyone could choose what to wear. But she warned, the other kids in school always seemed to know who was from the orphans' home, stamping everyone with a stigma we couldn't escape.

After supper, she said, Mrs. Swind would give us the clothes we'd need for school and tomorrow we'd be given our assignments for chores: kitchen duty, which might be any number of things, from peeling potatoes, to washing dishes; setting the tables for meals; or cleaning the bathrooms, or dust mopping the dorms, or ironing or mixing yellow coloring into the margarine. The list seemed to go on and on.

Alicia mentioned the word "demerits." I didn't know what that meant, but it sounded like some kind of punishment system. I didn't ask for details. There was so much to take in. Learning all the rules in order to avoid punishments seemed impossible. This sure was going to be a lot different from living at home. Would we be able to get used to all the rules, sleeping in single beds, doing chores so we didn't get punished? I worried about learning the names of the other twenty-six girls and about getting used to Mrs. Swind.

Alicia had whispered to me that Mrs. Swind had been in the army. I wondered if she had been a general and so thought we were supposed to be little soldiers, following her rules. My big question though, was whether I would be given permission to play the piano in the living room.

In bed that first night, I prayed in Italian as my Dad had taught me with Psalm 4:8. It was like a preamble: "In peace I will both lie down and sleep; for thou alone, O Lord, makes me dwell in safety." My parents did not like the bedtime prayer most kids were taught. It began: "Now I lay me down to sleep,.." and ended, "if I die before I wake." They both agreed that Psalm 4:8 was more appropriate for us children.

Then I prayed for Momma, Daddy, Rosalie, David, Ronnie, Doris, Charlotte, Baby Fran and me. I always prayed for my family in our birth order, with me last instead of first. I prayed the boys would be with us soon and that Momma would get well so we could all go home and be a family again.

Finally, feeling too alone in the bed without my sisters breathing next to me, I fell asleep.

Blue Bird Cottage

CHAPTER THREE

SUBMITTING TO MRS. SWIND

*T*he orphanage normally placed children under the age of five in the cottage for pre-school children, called Jack and Jill. Charlotte should have been assigned there, but Daddy had insisted that we stay together. Our first night at the orphanage, Mrs. Swind told Rosalie and me that we would be responsible for taking care of our little sisters. That was no different from the way it was at home where Rosalie and I had always been expected to take care of our younger sisters and brothers. I soon learned, though, that many things would be different at the orphanage.

When it was almost time for supper, Mrs. Swind told us to wash our hands and line up single file to march into the dining room, where she assigned our seats. We four huddled together in line, expecting that we would sit together, but Mrs. Swind separated us, keeping Charlotte and me at the table closest to her and sending Doris and Rosalie to a table in the corner.

I wondered why she wanted me close to her. Her eyes scanned the room, as if she were looking for someone to chastise. I was already suspicious of her, having noticed that most of the girls kept their distance and avoided any eye contact with Mrs. Swind.

Everyone called her "Mother Swind," but that didn't feel right to me. I had a mother, after all, and besides, Mrs. Swind didn't act very motherly.

At that first meal she told me, "Jerry, all the girls must learn to cut their own meat, but I think you will need to help your little sister until she is able to do that for herself." I nodded.

She responded sharply. "Don't nod your head. Answer me."

"Yes, Mrs. Swind, I'll help Charlotte."

Already I had angered her. I would need to be careful to do what she expected of me.

Charlotte and I sat stiffly at our places, not sure what to do next. All the other girls were staring silently at their empty plates, as if afraid to move. After several tense moments, Mrs. Swind asked one of the girls to thank God for our food. We were used to praying before we ate. Mom and Dad had us take turns saying grace. Still, at the orphanage even praying felt so different from home.

After we said grace, Mrs. Swind chose a girl from each table to be the server. These girls went to the kitchen and brought back large bowls of mashed potatoes, meat loaf, and green beans, plus a basket of bread for the table. Of course, there was no Italian bread, just the "American" kind, which tasted like cotton to us Messinas.

At home supper was usually some kind of pasta, plenty of Italian bread, and hearty soups with tiny bits of pasta in them called "*pastina*" or "*pippirini*." In spring and summer we had salads of lettuce and tomatoes from Dad's garden. Our favorite supper in winter was soup, pasta, and Italian bread.

This new American food at the orphanage might be difficult to get used to, but we didn't complain. There was plenty on the tables. At least it seemed we wouldn't go to bed hungry as we sometimes did at home.

After supper, Alicia warned us about the poached fish on Fridays, and that Mrs. Swind would force the children to eat it. If we didn't, we'd have it for breakfast the next morning. My siblings and I were used to the delicious deep-fried fish Daddy bought already cooked for our supper on Fridays.

Charlotte was a finicky eater and I was afraid she would not eat the fish. Rosalie and I took her aside and tried to explain the consequences if she did not obey. She could be very stubborn and we were certain she would defy Mrs. Swind. I worried about this all week. It would be terrible for all of us if Mrs. Swind removed Charlotte from Blue Bird and sent her to Jack and Jill Cottage.

That Friday, the disgusting fish was served and Charlotte just sat and stared at it, shaking her head. I had been assigned to kitchen duty so couldn't stay to help or coax her to eat. I kept glancing into the dining room to see Charlotte still sitting there with a sullen expression on her face.

Almost two hours went by. Then Mrs. Swind took a forkful of fish and tried to force it into her mouth. Charlotte made a face, tears streaming, her lips tightly closed. To my horror, Mrs. Swind slapped her across the face. Charlotte vomited on her plate and began to cry, "I wanna go home."

Merciless, Mrs. Swind shouted, "You must learn to obey! You must eat what is on your plate." She slapped Charlotte again, then pushed her toward the kitchen, where she had seen Rosalie and me watching. Angrily she ordered, "Jerry, get her out of here. Bathe your sister and put her to bed."

Doris, Rosalie, and I were heartbroken to see Charlotte treated so horribly. We didn't let Mrs. Swind see us crying, for fear she would punish us, too. We now understood why the girls were so afraid of her. I was shocked. At home Mom would never slap us or force us to eat. I tried to comfort my sister, "Daddy said we won't have to stay here for long." At that early stage, I really believed it.

That first night in the orphanage, Charlotte and Doris had been afraid to sleep in their dorm without Rosalie and me nearby. The dorm for older girls was on the other side of the cottage.

I heard Janice, one of the older girls tell Mrs. Swind, "The new girls, Charlotte and Doris, are crying because they want to be with Rosalie and Jerry." Mrs. Swind responded in a loud voice so that everyone in the cottage could hear. "They'll get used to it. Tell them to stop crying or I will come in there and give them something to cry about." There was no sympathy from Mrs. Swind. I prayed extra long that night, "Please, make Momma well so we can go home soon."

Mrs. Swind told us we'd have medical exams before going to school to ensure that we were not carrying infectious diseases that could be spread to other children. Young doctors in training came regularly from the free clinic to examine the orphanage children and sometimes placed us in a study they were doing. We four girls were given a regimen of vitamins and cod liver oil every morning to counter our malnutrition. The exams were done in the Infirmary next to the administration building. Any girl who was in a contagious state was kept in the Infirmary until she was no longer likely to give her disease to others. Mrs. Swind was constantly telling us to wash our hands to keep from catching a cold or flu.

Whenever we needed medical attention at home, Mom took us to the Free Dispensary, or welfare clinic. Sometimes she had to take all of us kids with her, not just the sick one, because there was no money for a babysitter. I always hated to go to the dispensary because it was such an ordeal for all six of us to take the streetcar or bus and then walk a half mile or so to the clinic. There we would wait for what seemed like hours, our feet dangling from the uncomfortable bench in the waiting room. There were no magazines or children's books to read.

The young doctors at the orphanage were friendly and seemed to enjoy talking with us. Once a doctor asked when he was measuring my height, "Have you always been this short?" I laughed and so did he. I knew he was trying to help me relax for my medical exam, but it was true that I was small for a twelve year old. I weighed eighty- five pounds and stood four feet ten inches tall almost my full adult height.

On my second day in Blue Bird, I screwed up my courage and asked Mother Swind if I could practice on the piano in the living room. To my surprise, she nodded yes. "I was told that you played well, so let's hear what you can do."

I did not have my music with me, but Mrs. Swind found an old book of hymns and asked if I could play any of them. I chose one and began to play. She seemed impressed that she could recognize the hymn.

"My music books are still at home," I told her, "but maybe my father can bring them when he comes to visit on Saturday. I will have to write him." She said I could use the phone to call him instead. When I told her we didn't have a phone at home, she offered me writing paper and a stamp, a kind gesture, at last, I thought.

The other girls were awed at my privilege—being allowed into the living room to play the "good" piano. I learned later that when Daddy was making arrangements for us to go to the orphanage, he'd insisted that I be allowed to practice on a good piano and to continue my weekly lessons at Mrs. Myrtle's house on the south side of Syracuse. I was grateful that he had arranged for me to continue what he knew I loved, my music. None of the other girls were given permission to leave the orphanage to go downtown alone, as I was for my lessons.

Gradually, my sisters and I learned Mrs. Swind's rules. Demerits were given for disobeying and demerits meant losing privileges. Her favorite punishment was to deny a girl the privilege of going outdoors to the playground. That was bad enough, but I was afraid she might keep us from seeing our father. For serious punishments, I worried we might be denied a visit home, even though the social worker had assured us we could go home some weekends. We might even be denied receiving visitors, I feared, if we ever had any. That seemed especially cruel to me, not being allowed to see any friends or relatives who might come. We learned that on some Saturday afternoons a movie was shown in the auditorium of the administration building, but that if we were under punishment we couldn't go. Our dad hadn't allowed us to see movies, so the prospect of a Saturday afternoon movie was exciting. I made up my mind to not earn too many demerits.

One of the major rules was doing our assigned chores correctly and quickly. If we took too long to mop, wax, and polish the black linoleum floors, we would be given demerits. If the clothes we ironed still had wrinkles or creases, more demerits. If Mother Swind found dust balls under the beds after we had dusted, demerits.

She demonstrated how to make a bed using what she called "hospital corners."

"The sheets cannot be pulled out at night if the bed is made in this special way," she barked. On Saturday mornings, we were to put the bottom sheet into the laundry. Then the top sheet would become the bottom sheet and we'd use a fresh sheet for the top. She checked our beds after we changed the sheets each week to be sure that we had used hospital corners, that there were no wrinkles on the white seersucker bedspreads, and that no blankets or sheets were hanging too far down.

If any of us forgot our chores, or if our work didn't pass inspection—more demerits. When a girl had ten demerits, she lost certain privileges. Girls would be denied dessert after that evening's meal or perhaps for a week, or would be sent to bed right after supper, denied a home visit, given extra chores to do, or prevented from seeing the Saturday movie, usually a cowboy serial.

I was especially afraid that I might be denied access to the piano. I couldn't imagine how I would survive without my music. Playing the piano was how I escaped when I felt sad, or when I was angry and knew I couldn't show it. Music was my refuge, my way of entering a world where life was perfect and beauty was everywhere.

In that world, I had no burdens and no responsibilities.

Somehow I would have to do everything "right" and not talk back to Mother Swind. But sometimes Rosalie and I muttered under our breath, hoping she couldn't hear us, complaining about her harsh rules and cold-hearted ways.

One of our chores as older girls was to bathe the younger ones before bedtime, and in the morning we'd help them get washed and dressed before school. We had to help them make their beds and we would get demerits if they didn't do well. I was old enough to understand that the punishments were meant to maintain order in a potentially chaotic situation, but I still found the system very difficult and demoralizing.

Charlotte and Doris were confused by all the rules, and I often found them crying. They were afraid of Mother Swind and very homesick. We all were, but Rosalie and I, being older, were better able to cope. We tried to comfort and reassure Doris and Charlotte.

"We're here with you, so you aren't alone. We'll be going home as soon as Mama comes home from the hospital."

We didn't know then that the orphanage would be our home for many years.

About three weeks after we arrived at the orphanage, Rosalie spotted David and Ronnie while walking home from school. She ran up and hugged them, then asked when they had arrived at the orphanage and which cottage they were in.

Rosalie hurried home to Blue Bird to tell me. "Good news! Ronnie is in Hiawatha and David is in Tigris Patrol!" David had told her that when a space opened up in Hiawatha, he would be joining Ronnie there. We were excited to share the news with Charlotte and Doris.

One of the older girls reported this encounter to Mother Swind, who found Rosalie and scolded her. "Don't you know you are not allowed to talk to any boys?"

Surprised, Rosalie answered, "But they're my brothers."

"Not even your brothers!" said Mrs. Swind.

I was outraged, but didn't know where to turn to complain, without getting punished myself.

That night I prayed even harder and longer than usual, though the refrain was the same as always. "Please God, make Mom well so we can all go home and be a family again."

Mrs. Swind had a special punishment for talking after lights out. She would force the girl to stand next to her bed, holding her arms out at shoulder height. When the poor girl's arm began to droop from fatigue, Mrs. Swind would swat them hard with a yardstick. If the girl cried, Mrs. Swind would hit her harder.

Rosalie had always been a talker, and one night Mrs. Swind came in and grabbed her out of bed. I heard Rosalie crying as she was dragged down the stairs. I heard the door to the cellar open and close, then no other sound. I couldn't sleep for worrying.

The next day Rosalie told me that Mrs. Swind had snarled, "This will teach you not to talk after lights out." Then she closed the door, leaving Rosalie crying alone in the cold, dark cellar.

Rosalie had been wearing only a nightgown made of handkerchief-thin cotton and no slippers. Soon she heard a noise, someone coming into the furnace room from outside. Frightened, she began sobbing, then realized it was the custodian who stoked the furnace at midnight.

She told me how gently he spoke to her, saying, "Little girl, what are you doing here?" That rare kindness made her cry so hard she couldn't speak. He called out to Mrs. Swind that he'd found a girl in the cellar who should be in bed. He must have guessed what happened and scolded Mrs. Swind, threatening to report her to Administration.

Rosalie was grateful he'd helped her, but still shaken as she told me the tale with the familiar frightened look in her squinty eyes. She was afraid Mrs. Swind would still find a way to punish her. I offered my usual reassurances. The next day the story went around the orphanage, about how the furnace man had rescued Rosalie and reported Mrs. Swind to the Administrator. She never sent anyone to the cellar after that, and we girls considered it a small victory over tyranny.

Another of Mrs. Swind's diabolical punishments, maybe the most humiliating one, was to force an offending girl to scrub down the stairs with her toothbrush. She would threaten, "If you put too much water on the stairs, you will have to lick it up." I never saw Mrs. Swind force anyone to do that, but the threat was enough to keep us all scared of her.

Our cottage had no TV yet, only a radio in the kitchen that the cook listened to. The only books in the study bookcase were old classics: *A Tale of Two Cities*, which I had already read in school, Longfellow's poems, a set of Nancy Drew mysteries, several old hymnbooks, and about a dozen books of camp folk songs. There were a few bibles, the old King James Version.

At home we didn't have many books, but Mom would take us to the library and encourage us to read. She liked to read but rarely had time for it. The only book Daddy ever read was his Bible. He used it like a dictionary when he wrote letters to his sisters in Sicily. When he needed to know how to spell a word, he remembered what verse it was in and looked it up in his Bible. Daddy also read the newspaper, following the reports of the war in Europe. He seemed to want to relive his First World War experiences sometimes, showing us on a map where he had fought in France, Belgium and Germany.

On the first Saturday that Daddy came to visit, he parked the Mondo Construction truck in front of our cottage. Charlotte and Doris noticed it first and called to Rosalie and me.

"Daddy's here! He wants us to come out to the truck." We ran out to see him. He had opened the door to the truck and was sitting sideways on the seat, his feet on the runner. He smiled broadly as we gathered around him.

His first question was, "Did you go to school yet?"

We all talked in a rush, telling him about school and our medical exams, the strange food and the other girls. We showed him our new play clothes and shoes. He admired them and seemed delighted as he listened to us. As he often had at home, he asked, "Are you being good children?"

We assured him we were, and naturally didn't tell him about Charlotte's refusal of the fish and Mrs. Swind slapping her, afraid he would blame all of us and scold us for not "being good."

Rosalie asked about Baby Francis and Daddy told us he was in a different foster home from where he had been. He said that after he left us he would be going there to see the baby of our family.

I asked about Mom and he told us, "I'm going to see her tomorrow and I'll ask the doctors when she can come home. God willing, it will be soon." I was relieved at his words, but also skeptical. We seemed to be all caught up in circumstances beyond our control.

"Daddy," I asked, "did you remember to bring my music books?"

He smiled. "Here they are. You keep practicing, you hear me?"

"Yes, Daddy, I will."

I leafed through the stack of sheet music he handed me. Glad to see my favorites again.

On some Saturdays, Daddy asked permission to take us out for an ice cream cone, but usually we visited with him for about half an hour by the side of the truck. Then he would be off to see Franny.

The night of that first visit, I prayed hard, as usual, but was beginning to wonder if we would ever live together as a family again.

CHAPTER FOUR

My Music

*G*radually we settled into the routine at the orphanage. We did our chores in the morning, lined up to walk to school, stayed there from eight until two-thirty, walked back, and changed our clothes. We did our homework and then more chores. Only then did I have time to practice my music.

Every day I looked forward to being alone in the living room, where I played the good piano. I especially enjoyed being out from under the watchful eye of Mother Swind. She seemed to always hover over us, waiting to catch someone breaking her rules so she could award another demerit. Unlike the others, I had an escape. Rosalie was also allowed to practice in the living room, so we had to negotiate who would practice before supper and who after.

Beethoven, Brahms, Bach, and Gershwin became my friends. I had a recurring fantasy that I was performing for them. I would picture myself sitting next to Beethoven, and though I knew he could not hear me, I felt that somehow he sensed I was presenting "Moonlight Sonata" just for him. What wonderful moments I had with my favorite composers, who were now my friends. My only other companions during those practice hours were Gainsborough's *Blue Boy* and *Blue Girl*, who hung on the walls near the fireplace. Occasionally, I looked up to see the wind blowing Blue Girl's skirt or the feather in Blue Boy's cap.

I tried hard to play each piece the way Mrs. Myrtle had when she introduced me to it. I wanted to bring the same power to the crescendos that she created. I loved hearing her play and yearned to perform with the confidence she had.

Helene Myrtle was a tall, handsome woman who wore heavy

makeup. She rouged her cheeks and always wore bright red lipstick. Unlike most women I knew, she had her hair done every week at a salon. She was always well dressed, usually in a suit, and wore fashionable high-heeled shoes.

Every year Mrs. Myrtle held a whole week of recitals during June, and at each one she glided out onto the platform wearing a different evening gown. Rosalie and I tried to guess which gown she might wear—the gold brocade, the blue silk, or the green velvet. They all shimmered beautifully in the subdued light of the recital hall. We were impressed that she had so many gorgeous clothes and considered her an elegant model of a successful woman.

Mrs. Myrtle took her job as music teacher seriously, yet she was kind and patient with her pupils. I never heard her scold anyone for not practicing, and she gave all her students their full share of her attention. With her own fine musicianship and her encouraging demeanor, she made us want to please her with our playing. Only occasionally would she pronounce "well done" when I finished a piece, I never felt belittled or neglected.

In a city where everyone locked their doors, hers remained unlocked during the day. Pupils would let themselves into the house and wait in her sitting room until she came out of the living room, which served as her studio. There was a red and blue oriental rug on the floor of her sitting room, two comfortable chairs, a potted plant, and the busts of two composers looking down at me from the bookcase. I loved waiting in that cozy room and listening to the piano sounds coming from her studio.

She patiently taught me music theory—dominant chords, minor chords, and chord progressions—explaining the universal structure of music. She helped me understand that it is not enough just to play the notes, that a musician must understand the way a composer organized themes to accomplish his intentions, like using minor chords to show sadness or a subdued mood and dominant chords to convey action and strength.

I took it all in deeply enthralled as Mrs. Myrtle told me stories about the great composers, the details of their lives that affected a particular composition. The previous year I had been amazed to learn from her that Beethoven became deaf during his later years and could not hear what he was composing, yet continued to write music. How could a deaf man compose such beautiful works? He must have heard it in his head, Mrs. Myrtle reasoned, remembering how each of the instruments sounded.

When I was thirteen, she asked me to perform every night during the week of recitals. I realized then that I was one of her star pupils. I was pleased that both Daddy and Aunt Fay came to every performance, but I missed Mom a lot on those evenings.

At the orphanage, I enjoyed playing scales and the special exercises Mrs. Myrtle gave me to stretch my small hands so that I would be able to play more advanced works later on. She never said my hands were too small, just that these exercises would "strengthen my reach." Sometimes when I was bored at school I focused on the music in my head and stretched my fingers on the desk as if I were at the keyboard doing my exercises.

Not long after moving into the orphanage, I was asked to play hymns for the church services that were held in the auditorium each Sunday afternoon. I was happy to do it; I was a pretty good sight-reader and most of the hymns were simple to play. However, church services at the orphanage were far from worshipful. The visiting ministers always talked down to us kids. When the preaching went too long, they would whisper, tell jokes, giggle, and slam the wooden folding chairs to make distracting noises.

Occasionally the visiting minister asked me to play hymns selected by the children, and sometimes singing these special songs calmed things down. When I made mistakes the kids glared at me, made faces, and giggled. Later they teased me, "You made those mistakes on purpose, didn't you? Just so church would end sooner, right?"

I always denied it, but it was true that my mistakes at the piano probably hastened the end of church for that particular Sunday afternoon, a relief for all of us.

During kitchen duty, I would work alongside the orphanage cook, Millie. Over the weeks and months, I heard her story and grew to admire her strength. She had left an abusive husband, cleaning houses to support herself and her daughter. To improve her lot, she took courses at the community college, which qualified her for the cook's job. Hearing about her college experience made me realize that I might be able to get a college education, too.

While I did my assigned chores, Millie would talk to me about how to cook American dishes. I'd open the large cans of vegetables with a manual can opener, pour the milk, peel vegetables, and mix the yellow coloring into the margarine—all the while taking in the story of this remarkable person who talked with me as an adult, not as an ignorant child.

Millie often told me how much she enjoyed listening to me practice the piano and asked what I had been playing. I was pleased that someone was that interested in my music and began to look forward to kitchen duty and the time I had with my new friend, Millie.

Shortly after arriving at Blue Bird, I made another friend. Helen was the daughter of the housemother at Blue Bell cottage next door. Helen and I were in the same classes and liked to walk to and from school together. We talked about nearly everything: our school work, our classmates, the kids we admired, and our favorite teachers. But I never confided in her about my mother in the mental hospital. Silence, shame, and secrets were the unspoken code for me and for most of the kids at the orphanage.

Aunt Fay was the only person I could talk with about my mother, but I did not see her very often. I don't recall her visiting us at the orphanage, but occasionally I would walk to Grandma's house after my piano lesson and on those visits I would talk with Aunt Fay. She was my mother's oldest sister, the only one of the five girls in the family who hadn't married. After Grandpa died, she had remained at home to support Grandma.

Aunt Fay had black wavy hair similar to my mother's. She complained about her Roman nose, but I thought she was attractive. She dressed almost as well as Mrs. Myrtle for her work as the secretary and bookkeeper in a plumbing store. She didn't wear suits as Mrs. Myrtle did, but had lots of fashionable dresses and shoes with two-inch heels.

The bathroom at Grandma's always had delicious fragrances of powder and cologne that I knew were Aunt Fay's. She talked softly, never raising her voice, and was very respectful of her mother. Aunt Fay played the piano, too, but admitted to me that by the time I was fourteen I had surpassed her.

On one of my visits, Grandma was in the kitchen cooking,

as usual, while Aunt Fay and I talked in the sitting room. She told me she wished she could visit Mom, but she had no transportation. She just shook her head when I suggested she could go with Daddy, confirming my sense that the two did not get along very well. I remember hearing a conversation in Italian she'd had with Grandma, blaming Daddy for Mom having so many children, implying that he was responsible for Mom's hospitalization. How much more did she know about our family? Was she aware that Daddy sometimes beat Mom and us kids? I never asked her.

While Grandma continued preparing supper, I asked Aunt Fay, "Why do you think Mom is in the state hospital? She didn't seem sick to me."

Aunt Fay frowned, and said she didn't know, and lamented, "The doctors will only talk with your father. You know it's very important for her to have visitors and to receive notes and cards."

I began sending Mom cards.

During our second month at the orphanage, Daddy got permission to drive me to Marcy State Hospital for my first visit to Mom. How frightening and painful those visits would be! Even before we got to the front door of the huge building, I heard patients screaming, taunting, and yelling at us from the windows, begging us to get them out.

Once inside, a nurse with a huge set of keys walked us down long corridors through four locked doors until we got to Mom's unit. They brought chairs out into the hall for us, since there was no special room for visiting patients. I asked Daddy how much we should tell her about the orphanage and he said we should only talk about things that would not upset her.

After we had waited about twenty minutes, Mom appeared. She was very excited to see us and looked just the same as always to me. Her sweet smile had not changed. We kissed and hugged her, and in her soft voice she asked, "How are all my babies?" I knew what she needed to hear, and said it. "We are all fine, Mom. We have plenty of clothes and good food, but we miss your cooking, especially pasta with your special sauce and the Italian bread we used to have at home." I told her we liked our new school, but hated taking cod liver oil every morning.

She nodded her head. "I remember how difficult it was to get

37

you all to take cod liver oil when we were living at home."

Daddy handed her a banana and a Hershey bar—two of her favorite treats —and we watched her devour the chocolate. Dad had a smile on his face as she unwrapped that candy bar and ate it as fast as she could. As she started in on the banana I asked, "Mom, how are you?"

That's when she told me about her electro-shock therapy. "They strap me down to a table, attach wires and needles to my head, and then they turn on the electricity and my whole body jumps."

She said she screamed and yelled and tried to get them to stop the treatments, but that they wouldn't listen to her. "I sleep for a long time afterward and lose track of what day it is." I could not understand how these awful treatments were supposed to help her get well.

"Frank," she begged, "You got to tell the doctors to stop the electric shock, you got to get me out of here." I looked at his face and could see how upset he was, but he was trying to stay calm. He said, "The doctor told me this will help you and you can come home sooner." My father was caught in the middle. Mom still insisted, "It's not helping me, you got to get them to stop!"

The worst part of the visit was when we started to leave. As we tried to kiss her goodbye, she began to beg us, at first quietly, then gradually working to a high-pitched scream. "Take me home! I want to go home! My children need me! Don't leave me here, I want to go home!" She kept shouting and threw up her arms, terribly angry. I glanced back as we walked away down the long corridor and saw her dragged, kicking and screaming, back into the locked ward. We could hear her cries all the way out to Mr. Mondo's truck, which would take us back to Syracuse and the orphanage.

Her demands made me feel as if I had some power to free her. Of course I didn't, but I still felt guilty for leaving her behind. I could not understand why we were free to walk out of the hospital but she was locked in. I could tell from Daddy's face that he felt as helpless as I did. I felt sick to my stomach but forced myself not to cry. Neither of us said a word on the long drive back to the orphanage.

I never told my friends at the orphanage about my visits to Mom. For several days after I remained very quiet and avoided talking with anyone except my sisters. I spent more time at the piano, losing myself in the music of Brahms or Schubert. My music in the living room at Blue Bird became a refuge from the knowledge that my mother was in a state hospital receiving terrible treatments and I could do nothing to save her.

My prayer became more insistent than ever — Please God, heal my mother so we can go home soon and be a family again.

Shortly after my fourteenth birthday, Aunt Fay got permission from the orphanage administrator to take me to my first concert at Lincoln Auditorium in downtown Syracuse to see Arthur Rubenstein, the famous pianist. I ironed my best Sunday dress two times to make sure every wrinkle was smoothed out. Feeling very special, I crawled into the taxi that Aunt Fay had ordered for us. I felt proud and waved to the other kids as the taxi drove away from Blue Bird.

When we walked into the auditorium, there was a lot of murmuring as people found their seats. Aunt Fay had gotten us seats on the left side of the concert hall so we could see Rubenstein's hands on the keyboard. As we waited for him to come on stage, Aunt Fay said, "You know, he carries his piano wherever he performs."

I pictured his piano on his back and asked, "How can he do that?"

She laughed. "No silly. I meant that he takes it with him. He doesn't like to play a different piano for every concert, so his own piano is shipped to the city where he will be playing." How important he must be, I thought.

There were over a thousand people in the auditorium, yet when the lights began to dim, the room fell silent. All eyes were on the stage as Mr. Rubenstein walked slowly across it. The audience applauded wildly even before he played a note. He sat down, moved the cushioned seat, swished the tails of his tuxedo jacket behind him. Then the audience abruptly stopped applauding and seemed not to breathe as he lowered his hands over the keyboard and began playing Beethoven's Appassionata Sonata. The moment his hands touched the keys I felt the beautiful sound pierce my body.

He seemed to forget the audience and the auditorium as he performed. When he finished a piece, he held his hands still over the keyboard for a few moments, until applause exploded like thunder. At the end of the evening, people were so ecstatic that they stood up and continued to clap and yell as he bowed several times. Many audience members shouted, "Bravo!" and "More, more!"

It was a thrilling and inspiring evening, and on the drive home I decided to devote more time to the piano so I could one day achieve the level of Rubenstein's perfect performance. I understood from my own experience playing at recitals how easy it was to be enveloped by the music and forget there was anyone listening. I loved getting lost in the music as Mr. Rubenstein had and began practicing longer hours, especially on weekends.

More and more, music became a major source of joy in my life.

CHAPTER FIVE

AN UNUSUAL
PERFORMANCE

*D*uring Daddy's Saturday visits, my siblings and I swarmed around him, clamoring for attention. He would focus on one or another of us for a time while the rest milled about, giving us a chance to catch up with each other. This is how I learned of the abuses in Hiawatha and Tigris Patrol.

David, who was only eight at the time, didn't want to tell Daddy, but he confided to Rosalie and me about Rufus Parker Potter, the house father at Tigris Patrol, beat him every chance he could. He said a large poster of Hitler was pinned on a closet door, and that Mr. Potter used it to threaten the boys, telling them he would bring Hitler to punish them. David described how Mr. Potter sat in his rocker with his feet up, a whip in his right hand, a cigar in his left.

"He reminds me of an animal trainer in the circus cracking his whip to scare us," David said. "He never calls me by my name, only 'Dirty Wop' or 'Dago'!" We never let Daddy know about Mr. Potter because we were afraid he might pick a fight or something worse—we didn't know what.

I felt sorry for David, and realized it was a lot harder for him than it was for us girls. We were punished, but we were not beaten. I tried to reassure him with my usual refrain: "It won't be long. We'll be able to go home as soon as Mom is out of the hospital."

A few months later, Rosalie saw David run up to Ronnie on the way to school one morning. "Ronnie, guess what!" David crowed. "Good news! I'm moving to Hiawatha after school today, we'll be in the same cottage!"

Ronnie was excited, too. "I'm going to ask if you can have the bed next to mine!"

Rosalie said they were hugging each other with delight. She asked them what was going on and couldn't wait to get home after school to tell Doris, Charlotte, and me.

I was so relieved that David would not be beaten any more by the housefather at Tigris. I didn't know then that the houseparents at Hiawatha also hit the boys. It was a long time before I found out. At the orphanage, we kept secrets from each other, as well as from Daddy.

Most of the kids at the orphanage did not talk about why they were there. We all were ashamed, knowing that some fathers were in prison, some mothers in a hospital —sometimes the state hospital, like our mother. When asked why we were living in the orphanage, most kids' answered "the war." Usually, though, we would eventually hear the truth from someone else.

David and Ronnie often said their Mom had died rather than tell anyone that she was in the state hospital, which would mean she must be crazy. How could they admit to that? More secrets.

During his visits, Daddy always asked if I was still practicing the piano. I told him about my upcoming recitals and he said he would attend. He gave me a couple of dollars to pay for the piano lessons for Rosalie and me. When I told him that Mrs. Myrtle had asked me to come to her house each week a little early to do some chores for her, he wanted to know what kind of chores.

"I wash out her nylon stockings and scour her kitchen sink. It's not difficult and she pays me each week."

He said, "That's good. Maybe pretty soon you can pay for your own lessons. If you keep it up, you could be a piano teacher when you grow up."

I agreed and told him, "Aunt Fay sometimes helps pay for my lessons, too."

He looked uncomfortable and said, "Yes, but that was supposed to be temporary."

To help ease the moment I said, "I'll try to get some baby-sitting jobs and maybe pretty soon I can pay for my own lessons."

The next Saturday morning I told Mrs. Myrtle, "My father wants me to be a piano teacher, just like you."

She smiled, "I can help you qualify for the Conservatory of

Music, where I graduated. Would you like that?"

I was hesitant, "Do you think I have the ability for the Conservatory? I know I would have to work hard, especially on the stretching exercises you gave me."

"Yes, I think you have the talent, but you would have to spend more time practicing. Of course, we still have several years to get you ready."

During my quiet time at the piano, I began to imagine what a career in music would be like. I might enjoy being a piano teacher, but some people seemed to think I was good enough to be a concert pianist. That's what some of the staff at the orphanage said although I wasn't so sure.

When Mrs. Myrtle had me play on each of the five nights during the recital week in June, I suspected that I was an advertisement for her skill as a piano teacher. It was wonderful that she liked my playing, but one night I proved that I was still very much a novice. I was playing Gershwin's Rhapsody in Blue from memory, when I got distracted. I began to daydream and realized a little later that I had played one movement twice. Mrs. Myrtle glared at me and I expected her to scold me at my next lesson. Instead, she reprimanded me in her usual quiet manner.

"You must keep your mind on your music, especially when you are performing." Then she changed the subject. "Would you like to play in a piano orchestra with thirty-two other pianos?"

I was surprised and relieved that she still trusted me after my major mistake.

She went on, "You will be the First Piano. In an orchestra, the first violinist is the concertmaster who plays one note that the other performers use to tune their instruments, so that everyone will be in the same key. Since the pianos will already be tuned to the same key you will not need to do that, but the conductor may call on you to demonstrate how he wants a passage to be interpreted."

Immediately I began to worry about not being able to follow him. Mrs. Myrtle continued, "There will be a whole program of piano pieces with some duets and even a piece with three students at each piano—99 children playing the 33 pianos. Do you think you can keep your mind on the music and not go wandering off?"

Naturally, my reply was, "Oh yes, Mrs. Myrtle!"

How exciting it would be to perform on the same stage where Arthur Rubenstein had recently given his concert. It was scary to know that I would be at the first, the main piano.

But I was thrilled that my teacher thought so highly of my playing.

Then she added, "I've chosen Rosalie to play in the concert, too. You'll be able to practice together at home."

What Mrs. Myrtle didn't know was that Rosalie and I often fought about practicing. I was jealous that she was horning in on my territory—my beloved piano. I often criticized her playing, certain that I was the superior pianist. Until the day of the concert, we fought and practiced and practiced and fought.

I knew several of the children who were to play in the concert. Barbara, my friend from church, was one of them. She was always encouraging me, telling me how she admired my ability to sight read almost anything that was put before me. Because I never felt very confident, her support was really important.

During the first rehearsal, my fear about being in such a prominent role melted away as I began to follow the conductor. He asked me to perform a passage to show the rest how it should be shaded: *pianissimo, allegro, or molto aggitatto.* My understanding of Italian helped me interpret the style he wanted. When he said, *"tempo di valse,"* I knew that meant waltz time for Strauss's *Blue Danube; "Molto sostenuto"* meant to play *Handel's Largo* in deliberate and very sustained manner, almost like a dirge. I could see from his smile that he was pleased with me.

The other students expected me to guide them the way a concertmaster does. Rosalie was at one of the other pianos until it came time to play the duet and trio, when she came and sat at my piano. It felt good having her close to me at "my" piano. At first she trembled, nervous to be sitting in the spotlight at the first piano, but soon she became lost in the music.

When I entered the stage on performance night, the auditorium was full and I felt anticipation in the air. My father, Aunt Fay, and my brothers were there, along with other friends of our family and a few from the orphanage staff.

When three of us played on the same piano, we somehow avoided jabbing each other in the ribs, but it was impossible not to feel constrained by the lack of space. The duets were easier, since we were not as crowded. The whole evening was a stirring experience for both Rosalie and me. For once my mind did not wander. I enjoyed being a concert pianist that one night, although I was uncomfortable with the eyes of so many people on me.

I was thrilled that my brothers, David and Ronnie, were allowed to attend the concert. Word got back to me that they later bragged to the other kids about their first concert and that their sisters were performers. Aunt Fay, Daddy and my brothers in attendance showed me that my family was still connected. Everyone said how proud they were of Rosalie and me and called us concert pianists!

The concert was repeated the following year, but with fewer pianos and with a city-wide orchestra and chorus. Rosalie played the cello, her first love, in that concert. Mrs. Myrtle wanted some of her other pupils to have the exciting experience so I did not play in the performance the next year. Unfortunately, too many logistical problems—moving and tuning so many pianos—prevented these wonderful children's concerts from becoming an annual event.

This once-in-a-lifetime experience was exciting, but I felt painfully shy and self-conscious when the spotlight was on me. I realized I did not want to be a concert pianist but still thought a career in music might be possible for me. I could become a piano teacher like Mrs. Myrtle, as Dad had suggested and help others find the joy and satisfaction that I had found in music.

Interestingly, it was Rosalie, not I, who eventually pursued that profession.

CHAPTER SIX

BELONGING

After I'd lived for a year at the Onondaga Orphans Home, a new social worker, Carlton Joiner, took over the administration. He was the first administrator with a Master's Degree in Social Work. He had modern ideas, and everything began to change.

Matrons like Mrs. Swind were replaced with a married couple to oversee each cottage. The husband would work in the outside world while the wife supervised the daily activities of the cottage. The couples seemed more like parents, and provided a more homelike atmosphere.

What a relief it was to see Mrs. Swind leave! She never said goodbye just carried her suitcase to the taxi and rode away, never to be heard from again.

The new house parents for Blue Bird were Mother and Daddy Wells. They both smiled a lot, and seemed very sympathetic, and were less severe in disciplining the girls. Mother Wells squatted down to be at the same level when she spoke with the younger children, using a soft voice and gentle manner. Daddy Wells had a degree in Forestry from Syracuse University and Mother Wells had taught school. Their own two children were grown.

Having become accustomed to Mrs. Swind's harsh ways, it took a while to adjust to Mr. and Mrs. Wells. One night just after we had finished dinner, we heard a plate smash while Edie was drying dishes in the kitchen. Everyone looked at Mother Wells, expecting her to be angry. Edie nervously apologized, "I'm sorry, it just slipped out of my hands."

Mother Wells just smiled and helped her pick up the pieces, saying, "Accidents do happen." We knew at that moment that our luck had changed. She was not like Mrs. Swind. She even asked us to help her as she learned her new position. An adult asking us for advice!

Hiawatha's new house parents were the Wilkes. Mother Wilke had blonde hair and was quite large; her husband—whom she called "Feathers"—seemed a slight man beside her. They were very jovial, and liked to tease and joke with the boys and even with us girls. Once, they invited Rosalie, Doris, Charlotte and me to a backyard cookout. We were delighted to have some time and a meal with our brothers and had fun playing badminton while Mr. Wilke grilled hamburgers, and his wife joined the kids in teasing and playing games.

But after a few months, Rosalie and I began to hear worrisome stories from David and Ronnie. They whispered to us on the way to school, telling us about how the Wilkes were mistreating the boys including our brothers spanking and even beating them.

My sisters and I couldn't help them but still agreed to keep this information from Dad, afraid that he would blame them and feel that they deserved the punishments. At home he had sometimes chased David and Ronnie with the razor strap. When they tried to hide from him he'd yank their arms and legs to pull them out from under their bed. He always had been quick to blame the boys and could be cruel, apparently forgetting they were small children.

Years later our brothers told us about sexual abuse they were subjected to by Mrs. Wilke. Everyone in our family had been continuing the secrecy that started long before my mother went into the state hospital.

When Francis arrived at Hiawatha at the age of three, after a succession of foster homes, the Wilkes spanked him almost every day for messing his pants. This continued for almost nine years until he was twelve or thirteen years old. No one considered there might be a physical or emotional problem that should be addressed. Many years later we came to the conclusion that his incontinence might have been caused by lactose intolerance, a problem for several of us Messinas.

The Wilkes would ridicule Francis, urging the other boys on. "Make fun of him! He can't get to the toilet and keeps messing his pants, just like a baby!" Mrs. Wilke forced Francis to wash his own underwear and hang it on the clothesline outside the cottage, where everyone could see it. Naturally, Francis was humiliated. He told me years later that he found a place to hide where no one would see him crying.

David told me when he was older that he knew he shouldn't let Mother Wilke get near him. She always seemed to want to touch and fondle the boys, or beat them for something whether they were guilty of it or not. To escape, David chose to spend most of his time outdoors whether it was summer or winter. Two Native American boys, Beaver and Chief, became David's friends in Hiawatha. They played softball or football on the playground or in the apple orchard behind. Another set of brothers, Teddy and Marshall, also played frequently with Ronnie and David and they, too, tried to avoid Mother Wilke.

It was several years before Mr. Joiner would learn of the physical and sexual abuse in Hiawatha. When he found out, he immediately dismissed the Wilkes, but not much changed when the Quackenbushes were hired. Mr. Q. had been a drill sergeant in the army. He appeared determined to discipline the boys the same way he had the men under his military command. The boys told us that he often beat them. Fran told us later that on several occasions he tried to keep Mr. Q. from beating some of the younger children, only to be whipped for interfering.

Not until Mr. and Mrs. Brandt became house parents at Hiawatha did Fran feel he could relax. There were no more beatings. They showed how much they cared for the boys by taking them on outings, and making special meals for them on their birthdays. The Brandts helped the boys with homework each night and took turns reading to the younger ones at bedtime.

There were quite a number of good additions at the orphanage after Mr. Joiner took over. Every child was assigned a Committee Woman—a church member who agreed to send birthday and holiday cards and small gifts to "her" child. Occasionally, a Committee Woman would take her child out for the day.

One of Fran's fondest memories were days spent with his Committee Woman, Mrs. Kaufman. He dressed in his Sunday clothes and although he was only nine years old, he said, " I felt like a little man." It was exciting for him to have such an outing where no one but Mrs. Kaufman knew he was from the orphanage and he could be the center of her attention. She took him to the zoo, to a children's movie or out for a snack.

He remembers the first time he ever ate in a restaurant. Mrs. K. told him he could select anything he wanted from the menu. When she realized he was overwhelmed with all the choices, she helped him choose a cheeseburger with French fries, which he said was just right.

Charlotte's Committee Woman, Mrs. Putnam, was faithful to her, too, paying attention to her for many years. She sent her dozens of cards, notes, and small gifts for her birthday and Christmas. Charlotte's face would always light up when mail arrived from Mrs. Putnam. Rosalie, Doris and I envied her. Our Committee Women seemed to change almost every year. We hoped to hear from them, but too often they forgot our birthdays.

Shortly after Mr. Joiner arrived he asked the residents of each cottage to choose two children to represent them in meetings with him. He said he wanted us to help him improve conditions in the institution. First, there should be a new name for "the home," he said, since there were no longer any orphans in the orphanage.

Rosalie and I were elected from Blue Bird. There were twelve of us kids at the first meeting, where Mr. Joiner said, "All of us around the table should take part in choosing a name. We can also discuss other changes that you would like to see."

I made a suggestion, "Maybe we should be called Hillcrest like the home in Rochester."

Mr. Joiner encouraged us to take our time. "Let's come up with a list of possible names and not just choose the same one as in Rochester."

He began to list some possible names on the blackboard and it did not take long for someone to suggest "Elmcrest." Tall elm trees surrounded the cottages and we all agreed that was a good choice.

Mr. Joiner was pleased, "I will present the name "Elmcrest" to the cottage staff and to the Board of Directors." He went on, "Now, what other changes should we consider?"

We all stared at each other, tongue-tied.

Finally, I asked, "Would it be possible for us not to have church in the auditorium on Sunday afternoons?" Heads nodded in agreement.

"Why is that a problem?" he asked, genuinely concerned.

Rosalie and I both contributed details, "Some of the ministers don't know how to talk to us kids. There is a lot of giggling, pinching, and misbehaving because it's hard to listen to these ministers. We like the singing, but some of the hymns they choose are too long."

Everyone nodded in assent.

Mr. Joiner said he might be able to do something about the situation, but asked us to give him a month or two to work on it. We all agreed to be patient.

The Staff and Board of Directors enthusiastically agreed to change the name of the orphanage to "Elmcrest Children's Center." Even the adults were excited and proud that we kids had had a part in the name change. At that time, it was unheard of to invite children to participate in such important decisions, but Mr. Joiner was firm in wanting to include us in developing a more open institution.

School personnel still referred to Elmcrest as "the home," but we all felt better about writing "Elmcrest Children's Center" on official forms rather than "Onondaga Orphans Home." Now we'd no longer have to explain that we were *not* orphans.

Mr. and Mrs. Joiner lived in a two-story home on the Elmcrest grounds and I soon began to baby sit for their two sons. The first time I went to their home to baby sit, Mr. Joiner saw me admiring the highly polished baby grand piano in the living room and invited me to play it. I was a bit shy and reluctant to sit at the elegant piano, but he coaxed, "Please, play something for Mrs. Joiner and me before we leave." I sat down and played the *Minute Waltz* by Chopin since it was brief and would not delay their plans for long. The piano was the most beautiful one I had ever seen and the sound filled the whole house. It was wonderful. When the Joiners urged me to play something else, I chose a Beethoven Sonata. What a perfect instrument for Beethoven's music, melodious yet strong. When I finished playing, they praised me effusively, and invited me to play their piano as much as I liked.

That first time I babysat for their boys was a real challenge. As soon as the parents left for the evening, they began chasing each other around the two-story house with kitchen knives. I was terrified that John, the nine-year-old, would seriously hurt

Jerry, who was only seven. I knew I shouldn't let them see how scared I was. I called to John, keeping my voice soft so he had to stop yelling to hear me. I carefully took the knives from their hands but did not return them to the kitchen where they might pick them up again, but instead placed them on a high shelf in the living room where I could keep track of them. The boys accused each other, "He started it," but I avoided taking sides.

"John, go to your own room, for ten minutes and no comic books until you have calmed down." "Jerry, you stay here with me." I quietly talked with Jerry about the danger of running with a knife in his hand, keeping my voice barely above a whisper. This seemed to help him calm down. When he had quieted, I told him he could have one of his books.

John called from the upstairs hall, "It's too early for me to go to bed."

"I will be up in a minute, John." As I started up the stairs, I determined how I would talk with him. "If you do not chase Jerry you can stay up another half hour, but if you do, off to bed you will go." I spent several minutes talking softly with John reminding him of the danger of running with a knife in his hand and how he could hurt his brother and himself.

When the Joiners returned from an evening out, we would talk about how things had gone. I would tell them everything that happened and they came to appreciate how I "managed" their boys. Telling me I was one of the few sitters who could do it. I was very pleased the Joiners recognized and respected my skills and entrusted me with their sons. They were more difficult than any children I had taken care of--nothing like my brothers, who'd never attack each other.

I was usually exhausted after sitting for the Joiners, but they paid me generously and I was pleased to have money that I had earned myself. Each week I earned enough to partially pay for my own piano lessons, the bus fare, and an occasional box of popcorn, which I ate while waiting downtown to change buses. Earning money helped me feel more independent.

A few months after our meeting with Mr. Joiner, he announced that we would no longer have worship services in the auditorium and that buses would take us to the large downtown churches on Sunday mornings.

The prospect of going to the downtown churches sounded exciting. Since Elmcrest was for protestant children, we all were assigned to different protestant churches. All of us Messina kids were assigned to Park Central Presbyterian Church.

When we told Daddy that we were going to church downtown, he frowned in disapproval. "You got your church in Solvay, where you grandpa Andrew helped to start, No? Did you forget?"

I explained, "The buses only go from Elmcrest to the downtown churches, it's a special project of the Council of Churches. Christian Assembly Church is in Solvay, too far away from downtown, the services there are in the afternoon. We don't have a way to get there."

Even before we had moved to the orphanage, we had begun to dislike going to our parents' church because the service was in Italian, which we did not understand. Afterwards, we kids would wait outside for our parents, and the neighborhood kids would taunt us calling us "holy-rollers." This seemed derogatory, but when we asked Mom what it meant she just told us not to pay any attention to them. I guessed they made fun of us because of the loud enthusiastic singing and praying in Italian that went on for hours.

But there were good things there, too. During prayer time, everyone confessed their sins which seemed to ease people's minds. The service was very cathartic for the Italian congregation, since many of them experienced a great deal of name-calling and prejudice during the week. The men talked about their bosses calling them "wop" or "dago." On Sundays they prayed for patience to stand up to insults and they prayed to change the hearts of their bosses to be more sympathetic to their needs. The hymns were usually sung in Italian, but when they sang in English we felt included.

When I was thirteen I began having fainting spells. After the first two of these spells in Blue Bird, I was sent to see a doctor who suspected I had either rheumatic fever or epilepsy.

He said, "To be on the safe side you will need to stay in Hygeia for a while for observation."

Hygeia was the name of the small hospital on the grounds behind Jack and Jill, the cottage for preschool children. Kids with infectious ringworm, chickenpox, and other diseases were quarantined at Hygeia.

A week later I was diagnosed with rheumatic fever and prescribed bed rest for the next three months, the usual treatment for rheumatic fever in those days.

The doctor's orders frightened me. "If you stay perfectly still and have no visitors, and if you do not walk around at all, you may be lucky and have no lasting heart disease."

What a blow, no visitors, and stuck in bed for the next three months? I could hardly believe it. What had I done to bring this on? I asked the nurse and she assured me, "You did nothing wrong. Some children just get it and it can have a long-term affect on the heart so it is very important that you follow your doctor's orders."

My homework was dropped off each week by someone from school, and my Dad was my only visitor. I tried to find out more about my condition but the doctor would only repeat his instructions. I asked Dad "What did the doctor tell you about why I'm here?" It was clear he didn't know any more than I did. I worried maybe there was some big secret that they were not telling me. But Dad only repeated the Doctor's instructions, "Stay in bed, no walking around, no visitors and rest for three months."

I read books and pretended to play the piano using the extra pillow as a keyboard. I missed my sisters and brothers and was terribly lonely and bored with nothing much to do but read. *The Tale of Two Cities, Little Women, Pride and Prejudice* became my favorites. I read *Little Women* twice, falling in love with Jo for her free spirit and her ability to get her sisters to cooperate putting on plays for their mother.

I prayed a lot, trying to understand what this illness would mean to me. Would I be able to live a normal life? Would I still be allowed to travel by myself to my piano lessons? I kept these thoughts to myself, but spent lots of time silently worrying.

What a great day it was when the doctor told me I could return to Blue Bird, my sisters, my piano, and school. But first, I would have to start walking around the hospital corridors to strengthen my legs. I was told I could no longer take Physical Education but the doctors said my heart would be okay. I returned to a near normal life. I still wondered about my heart. If I was normal why was I not allowed to participate in Physical Education? A few years later I learned that there was a notation in my school health record that I might suffer from epileptic seizures, but I never had a seizure, and I was never able to get the notation removed from my school records.

Everyone at Blue Bird had smiles on their faces as they welcomed me, especially my sisters, who hugged and kissed me. Mother Wells told me they all had missed me and were glad I was healthy again. Even the Joiner boys were glad to have me back.

At age fourteen I was attending high school and enjoying more freedoms, eagerly participating in after-school activities. I joined the Y-teens group of the YWCA and the Girl Scouts where I began to make friends with some of the girls from the wealthier neighborhoods near Elmcrest. I became interested in interior design as I prepared for my first Girl Scout badge. The Scout leader had taken us into several of the finest homes in Syracuse and explained the use of color in interior decorating.

"Notice the three dominant colors in that painting," she said. " See how they were used to select colors for the rug, draperies, sofas and chairs for a tasteful design?"

I was silent, absorbing the thick rugs, the beautiful silk sofas with contrasting colored pillows and the large elegant bathrooms. I had never seen anything like these beautiful houses and dreamed that maybe someday I could use the color formula to decorate my own home. What a wonderful fantasy—that I would grow up to live a normal life!

Through the Y-teen program we developed leadership skills, learning Roberts Rules of Order and how to conduct a meeting and make decisions democratically. Our group was made up of Jewish and Protestant girls. And we all decided to learn more about other faiths. (The Catholic Church would not allow girls to join the YWCA at that time.)

Two of my closest friends in Y-teens were the Flah twins, Jean and Joan. They were friendly and down to earth, and even though their parents were wealthy they were not arrogant or haughty.

One day they invited me to their home. Disbelieving I said, "Me? You want me to come to your home and meet your mother?"

"Yes, Mother wants to meet our friends, and you are our friend."

I was very moved by the warm welcome I received at their home. Their mother smiled a lot, was very friendly and suggested that I accompany them to their synagogue some time.

I did so and was fascinated with the way the Jewish prayer books started at the back rather than the front. I had never seen Hebrew writing before. Jean and Joan explained the meaning of the symbols in the stained glass windows—Noah and the ark, and Moses leading the Israelites out of Egypt. They said that their Holy Book was what we called the Old Testament. I knew about Moses and Noah, but all of us were surprised to discover we had the same favorite story, in which Ruth insists on traveling with her mother-in-law to a strange land after her husband dies. Ruth's words, "Wither thou goest, I will go." became our favorite inspiration and we found our faiths connected through the sacred texts and the Psalms. Jean and Joan became true friends, and I was so grateful they had not been put off by my living at Elmcrest.

In winter, my best friend, Helen and I, would trudge through deep snow to school. We'd stop at the bottom of Salt Springs Road to pick up Ann, another friend from school and church. Helen and I were known as the "gigglers" both at school and at church. When we were reprimanded, both of us would be called because it wasn't clear who was responsible for the giggling. Helen and I always had lots to talk about: our math homework, our friends at church and school, Y-Teens and Girl Scouts. Thanks to Helen and these groups I began to feel that I belonged. Finally, I had friends whom I cared about and who cared about me. They accepted me as I was.

My friendship with the Flah twins lasted (through correspondence) over ten years, and with Helen over fifty years.

Doris made close friends with Dawn and Delight Garafalo, the twins who lived next door in Marigold Cottage. Charlotte's best friend was their younger sister, Polly. They were Italian protestants who came from the northside of Syracuse as we did and also had a mother who was unable to care for them. They were in some of the same classes at school and went to our church with us. Knowing the Garafalos made us all feel a little less "different."

In high school, girls were required to take Home Economics where we were supposed to learn to cook and sew. I hated the sewing, I couldn't understand what making a laundry bag had to do with my life. The idea of learning to cook seemed silly. I was sure I already knew how to cook. After all, hadn't I been cooking for my family when we lived at home? I had to admit, though, at least to myself, that I mainly knew how to fix pasta.

When the Home Ec. teacher announced that we would learn to make cream of tomato soup, I was sure it would be easy and boring. She asked us to write down the recipe, and strictly follow the recipe which began with making a white sauce. My partner and I put the butter and flour in the pan, but when we added the milk it seemed much too thin. I decided that we must have copied the recipe incorrectly, and convinced my partner to use one cup of flour instead of one tablespoon. When we added it, the mixture turned as thick as library paste, and we started to giggle. We added the can of tomato soup, as called for, but of course the result was inedible. The teacher was furious with us for not sticking to the recipe. "You must have been daydreaming again," she scolded.

We tried to pour the glob of soup down the drain, but it was too thick. This set off our giggling again. We earned an F for that day, but I had learned a valuable lesson: When you don't know what you're doing stick to the recipe.

When I told Millie, the cook at Blue Bird, about my cooking disaster, she laughed and showed me how to make a proper white sauce, saying that we can always learn from our mistakes. She began teaching me to cook American food, and I soon stopped worrying about making mistakes. She even taught me how to turn my disasters into something edible, and how to use leftovers to create another meal. For example, the oily poached fish served in our cottage on Fridays could be turned into delicious fish chowder by adding liquid and celery, carrots, potatoes and onions. It was a new learning for me that with just a few ordinary additions, the dish could become so tasty, one we all enjoyed.

My sisters and I began to realize that Elmcrest was not such a bad place to live. There was always enough to eat, and we had plenty of clothes and shoes. We liked most of the kids we were living with, and our Blue Bird house parents, Mother and Daddy Wells, were fair, cared about us and were interested in our school work. All four of us Messina girls had developed important friendships and we began to feel at home at our new church. In summer we looked forward to going to Salvation Army camp on Lake Ontario with other kids from Elmcrest and with other children from foster homes in Syracuse.

We settled into a safe and comfortable routine: going to school and church with close friends and enjoying the special activities Elmcrest provided that we had never known at home.

Each summer Daddy Smith, the President of L.C.Smith Typewriters, would come to Elmcrest with a small truckload of watermelons. All the cottages would be informed, "Today is Watermelon Day!"

We'd gather on the playground around the truck and Daddy Smith and his driver would cut up and distribute slices of watermelon to all the children. Charlotte would astound all of us with how much watermelon she could consume. Unlike everything else there was no limit to how much anyone could have—as much as anyone wanted to eat. That was always a very happy day at Elmcrest.

There were other events like that throughout the year. At holiday time the Masons entertained all the children, gave each of us gifts and served us a turkey dinner. Then I would play the piano and we all would sing for the Masons and their wives.

CHAPTER SEVEN

THE ZAMPI FAMILY

*B*efore we lived in the orphanage we would visit my grandparents Sunday evenings, and we'd also see our aunts and uncles. Grandma Assunta, my mother's mother, always made pizza for us. We loved to watch her make the dough from scratch, adding tomato sauce or fresh tomatoes and cheese. Her kitchen smelled of rising dough and cookies baking in the oven. We all looked forward to Sunday evenings for our pizza, cookies, and stories. During these visits Grandma would tell about how she met Grandpa. Grandpa Andrew only wanted to read to us from his Bible. His English was not very good and it was boring to hear him read long passages so we were always eager to gather around Grandma while Grandpa was elsewhere reading his Bible. Aunt Fay or Mom would translate for Grandma.

This is what she told us: Grandpa Andrew (my mother's father) grew up in Rome, where he became an apprentice to a carpenter while still in his teens. Sometimes he would deliver barrels of wine to some of the large villas of the city. He looked forward to delivering to one villa where a young attractive girl, Assunta, lived. She was about fourteen. He was several years older. He would tell her stories of America, where he'd heard that young men could make lots of money, and he was planning to go there to work. Assunta was sure he was just trying to impress her. She did not believe his stories.

Assunta del Vecchio and her younger brother, Joseph, had been orphaned when they were ten and eight respectively. At that time the custom in Italy was for wealthy families to take in orphans who would become their servants. However, the wealthy woman who'd heard about Assunta and Joseph invited them to move into her home, assuring them she didn't expect them to become servants. The way Grandma told the story, the woman cared for Assunta and Joseph as if they were her own children. Her only request of Assunta was that she dust the leaves of the huge potted plants along the grand staircase of her villa each day, a chore that Assunta loved.

Andrew had followed through with his plan to go to America. Upon arriving in New York, he joined a group of men going to Scranton, Pennsylvania, to work in the coal mines. For two years he saved a large amount of money and returned to Italy to persuade Assunta to marry him. She refused, telling her brother, Joseph, that Andrew was a braggart. She could not believe such wild stories Andrew told her about America. She remained content to live in the villa with her brother under the wing of her wealthy guardian.

Determined to win Assunta's hand, he returned to Rome a second time and again tried to persuade Assunta to marry him. This time Assunta's guardian suggested that maybe she should consider marrying Andrew. She pointed out that he was resourceful, educated (indicated by his love of reading), and a hard worker. Clearly, he was enamored of Assunta, having made two trips to Rome with proposals of marriage. As she told it to me later, Assunta, my grandmother, believed that her guardian was hinting for her to leave the safe haven of the villa. Because women in those days had few choices in life other than marriage, Assunta felt trapped. She reluctantly agreed to marry Andrew, but first persuaded him to include her brother, Joseph, in their travel plans for America. The sting of the unwanted marriage was lessened knowing that at least she and her brother were going to stay together.

After a brief time in Scranton, Andrew moved the three of them from Pennsylvania to Binghamton, New York, and then on to Syracuse in upstate New York. He bought some land on the outskirts of Syracuse and began to build a fourteen-room house for their growing family. Assunta tried to persuade him to build a smaller house, fearing they'd have to fill all those rooms with more children than she wanted or felt they could afford, but Andrew persisted with his grandiose ideas. However, when the depression hit them, they lost the house and were forced to move to a rental in the southern part of Syracuse. By then they had seven children. Grandma Assunta never let Grandpa Andrew forget that if he had listened to her good advice they would still be home owners.

During his previous visits to America, Andrew had begun visiting protestant churches, convinced that the Catholic Church was taking advantage of people. He did not like the way the priests controlled parishioners' beliefs and told how much they should contribute to the church. Even the confessional was misused, and he particularly objected to priests who invited themselves for dinner at their parishioner's homes, taking advantage of their limited food budget. Andrew and a few of his friends collaborated to start an Italian Protestant church, and established it in the suburb of Solvay. They called their church "Christian Assembly" and eventually established a new denomination with Italian-language churches—primarily in New England, New York, and Pennsylvania.

Andrew studied the Bible diligently and taught it to his wife and children without the Catholic priest's interpretations. He began traveling to Albany, Boston, Springfield, and other cities to help establish similar churches among Italian immigrant communities. Assunta complained that he was usually away just when she was about to have another baby. He justified his trips by insisting, "I'm doing the Lord's work."

As the children arrived—two boys and five girls—he insisted that they not be named in the traditional Italian way after saints and parents. Andrew told Assunta, "We are no longer Catholic and we now live in a new land so we do not have to be bound by those outdated traditions."

Grandpa Andrew fell in love with the name Fanezia, a heroine in one of his treasured Persian novels, and named his first-born daughter after her. For a few years she was called Fanny, but Aunt Fay hated both names, and when she could, she had it legally changed to Fay. The oldest son was named Arnold. When the next daughter was born, she was named Almerinda, another name from a Persian novel. Almerinda, my mother, said she liked having a name no one else had. Her sisters and brothers called her Al.

The sisters, Almerinda and Fay, were very close. From grade school on, they walked to school together and both were excellent students. Fay was the kind of older sister Al could look up to. They genuinely enjoyed each other. Because of the way their birthdays fell, Almerinda and Arnold were in the same class in school. Sometimes Almerinda admitted holding back because she did not want to outshine her older brother. Grandpa Andrew turned to the Bible for names for the rest of their children, which pleased Grandma. There were three more girls, Rose, Mary, Rebecca, and the youngest child was John.

Almerinda thought her parents would be impressed when Frank, an older man from Italy, became interested in her. But her father, Andrew, was bitterly disappointed in Al when she became pregnant at fifteen. The custom then was for women to marry the baby's father, but Assunta and Andrew did not like Frank Messina. He was from Sicily and they believed nothing good came from Sicily except blood oranges. To make matters worse, he was thirty-five years old, twenty years older than Almerinda. But a compromise of sorts emerged when Andrew, her father, began to "educate" Frank, teaching him the Bible and Frank agreed to join the Italian Protestant church that Andrew had helped to found. Only then did Andrew consent to the marriage. He continued to teach Frank the Bible and the hymns of the church, and Frank became zealous in his new-found religion, preaching and witnessing to his mates at work.

Frank and Almerinda named the baby Angelo, after Frank's father. When the baby died two days after birth, Frank and Almerinda were devastated. Frank was convinced that God was punishing them. Grandpa Andrew reminded Frank he was still thinking like a Catholic. "But you are now Protestant. We believe in a loving God, not a vengeful God."

Almerinda was only sixteen, and still wanted to return to school, but at that time public school regulations did not allow married girls to continue their education. Instead of sitting at home, she found a job using her artistic talent at Syracuse China, where she hand-painted flowers, leaves, and birds on the plates of fine china, the only paid job she would ever have. Three years later when Almerinda was nineteen, I was born and the whole family celebrated. Almerinda's four sisters decided they would name the baby. Rose had heard that it brought good luck to a baby if their initials spelled a word. They put their heads together with Al and decided to name the baby Geraldine Eileen Messina, GEM. This time the father had no say in the naming.

I have many pleasant memories of visits to our grandparents when we were growing up. I always loved the way the bathroom smelled like flowers. I knew that the lilac fragrance was from the powder and cologne that Aunt Fay used, my first inkling that women used something other than soap and water. I wished that our bathroom had those scents, but I knew my mother could not afford such luxuries. When Aunt Fay hugged me, she exuded the same delicious fragrances. I wanted to grow up to be like her and to smell like her.

One time when Grandma was baby-sitting David and Ronnie, she asked them to empty the trash in the cellar. They were only five and six and they wanted to be helpful. They lit a match to burn the trash. When the flames began to hit the ceiling of the cellar, they cried for Grandma to come help. She yelled to Rosalie to call the fire department and the fire was soon extinguished. The firemen scolded the boys, who apologized for starting the fire, and then Grandma took her turn in Italian.

When we visited Grandma Assunta during the spring and summer, she would take us for walks to the nearby park. While we played on the swings and slides, she would take her kitchen scissors from her apron pocket and make cuttings from the plants in the park gardens. She'd root them in glasses of water on the window-sill in her kitchen, then plant them in pots that decorated her house. She knew she should not be clipping the shoots, and asked us not to tattle on her. In Italian, she said, "It's good for plants to be cut back a little, it helps them to grow stronger." Then she would tell us again the story of the huge potted plants that she'd dusted and watered in the villa where she had lived after she was orphaned. She loved to tell the story, and we loved hearing it.

Shortly after the 1941 Pearl Harbor attack by Japan, newspaper articles said that the U.S. government was considering sending German and Italian non-citizens back to their home countries. There were rumors that some Italians had already been detained like the Japanese in internment camps. Many years later, we learned that a thousand Italians had been sent to camps in various parts of the country, and some were confined to their homes. Our family was very concerned that Grandma Assunta could be sent back to Italy if she did not become a citizen. It became a family project to teach Grandma American history and English so she could pass the citizenship test. I helped her with basic English. She seemed eager to learn when the threat of leaving her family was impressed upon her. All of her children forced her to use English every day to prepare her for the test. What a celebration we had when she finally passed and received her papers declaring she was a naturalized citizen of the United States of America! I was disappointed that she promptly went back to using Italian and forgot most of her English.

Another time when I was visiting after one of my piano lessons, Grandpa Andrew asked me to fix his lunch. He wanted some green peppers and eggs, a family favorite. I assured him that I knew how to fry them but I was focused on listening to a radio program in another room. I lost track of the peppers and ended up burning them. Grandpa shook his head, "You are just like your mother and grandmother. Someone is always burning my lunch."

On Saturdays Grandma would take me to the farmers' market. I would watch her bargain with the farmers and enjoyed her delight when she got her price but I hated going on the streetcar with her when she bought a live chicken. She'd kill it in the backyard and enlist me to pick the feathers. When I asked why she did not buy one from the butcher, she said that was the way she always bought her chickens, and she knew they'd be fresh. I told her she was old-fashioned. She nodded her head in agreement. It was clear I would not change her ways. Another time she asked me not to wear shorts when I came to visit. I asked, "Why?" She said, "You embarrass your grandfather when you wear shorts." I complained, that he was old-fashioned, too.

"Yes, he still thinks that girls should only wear dresses. He did not allow any of his daughters to wear shorts, either."

I frowned, but agreed to comply. I could argue with my parents about such things but my mother had taught me to honor my grandparents' wishes.

Although no one seemed to know what had become of grandma's parents, I always had a special feeling for her, knowing that she had lost her mother and father at an early age. She had been an orphan and we Messinas had been sent to an orphanage when our mother was unable to care for us. Grandma never came to visit us at the orphanage. I wondered if it was too painful for her to remember her own childhood.

CHAPTER EIGHT

THE MESSINA FAMILY

*S*ince we never knew our Messina grandparents (our father's family,) the only information we had about our father's growing up years were from him and, occasionally, from his brother, Salvatore.

My father, Francisco Messina, was born in 1893, in the city of Canicatti in central Sicily, one of seven children, two girls and five boys. Although his father owned a small flock of sheep that their relatives envied, the family was still considered poor. In fact, his father had difficulty feeding his large family and encouraged his children to take oranges from the trees of his neighbors when they were hungry.

Francisco was one of the younger boys in the family. Each one had to take his turn tending the sheep until he was able to find a job where he could earn real money. When Francisco was in the third grade, his father ordered him to end his formal education. It was his turn to be the shepherd. He did not take his job seriously and sometimes lost track of a sheep or two earning merciless beatings from his father.

Francisco had a violent temper, too. When he was ten, he picked a fight with his brother, Salvatore, and sliced off his ear with the knife he always carried. After taking Salvatore to the hospital, their father and older brothers hunted Francisco for a day and a half. He hid in the fields but knew he could never escape the physical punishments that were meted out frequently by his father who had been raised the same way. That kind of violence is shocking now, but then it was more common, and it would become the way that Francisco would discipline his own sons when he became a father.

When our father told this story, it was clear that he regretted what he had done. He would tell us we should take care of each other and not to hurt our brothers and sisters. He reminded us that family was most important, it was "everything." He said Salvatore had forgiven him but it seemed to us that our father had never forgiven himself despite all the time that had passed.

When Francisco was nineteen, he had managed to earn enough money to buy a ticket for a ship that sailed from Palermo in Sicily to New York. His sister, Filomena, also went to New York City, where she worked in the garment industry until she could afford to buy a Singer sewing machine. She returned to Canicatti with her new sewing machine, and made her living as a dressmaker the rest of her life. She never married. Salvatore also migrated to New York, while a third brother chose Argentina.

The youngest sister, Calogera, lost her husband in World War I, and like other widows in Italy, wore black dresses the rest of her life.

According to the story, Francisco's first job in New York was as a dishwasher at the Waldorf Astoria hotel. Most of the dishwashers were newly arrived immigrants from southern Italy or Sicily and spoke a common dialect. They called each other "paisano," meaning a special friend from the same country. His new friends told him he should call himself, Frank, now that he was in America. From then on, he was Frank.

When he received his first paycheck, his cohorts insisted that it was customary to take them out for a drink. He was so naive that he used up all his money buying beers for his friends, a hard lesson for a new arrival. He told the story to us as a cautionary tale, a warning that we should be careful with our money and not be as trusting or naive as he had been.

In 1913 he was working with a crew on the railroad between Buffalo and Albany. One of the men asked him if he was related to another Messina he'd met whose name was Salvatore. This led to the reunion of the brothers. Despite what had happened as children, they were glad to see each other. After all, they were family, and to Sicilians family was everything.

With the money he earned, Salvatore bought property near the outskirts of Syracuse and married Concetta, a young woman who had recently arrived from Italy. Together they raised a family of three children. Oddly enough, Concetta was hospitalized at Marcy State Hospital where my mother was, and at the same time, although they did not see each other. After about a year, Concetta was released and returned to her family. It is curious that these two brothers both had wives who were hospitalized for mental problems. I discovered that a third brother also had a wife who spent many years in the local mental hospital in Sicily.

It had been a mystery why three of the brothers had wives who were diagnosed with mental illness. Perhaps, these brothers were brought up to be "crazy-makers." Placing pressure on their young wives to produce many children when they couldn't support them and the violence they experienced growing up may have been the ingredients that contributed to the wives' mental illness.

Despite these few stories, we know very little about my father's family. He did not talk about them, although I know that he corresponded with his sister, Filomena, and frequently sent large boxes of our discarded clothes to her to be distributed amongst family members. He couldn't correspond with his sister, Calogera, since she never learned to read or write.

During World War I Frank had fought for the United States, thereby earning his citizenship. At that time if you joined the United States army, you were eligible to become a naturalized citizen without taking a test. He was proud that some of his brothers were fighting in the Italian army, which was an ally of the United States.

Life in the muddy trenches during the war must have been unbearable. When we would ask my father about his experiences he would shake his head, pause for a moment and tell us a story. The men would get stuck in a trench for days, where the stench of dead bodies and excrement would be overwhelming. For months at a time, army rations consisted of beans. My father got so tired of eating beans for every meal during his military days that for the rest of his life he would not touch them.

He was particularly proud of having carried his Captain, a man he greatly admired, on his back for many hours to the army's makeshift hospital tent near the front. He did not steal anything from his pockets as was frequently done by others when they found a wounded or dead soldier. Many years later he was reunited with his former Captain, who again thanked him warmly for saving his life.

While Francisco was tramping across France with his infantry division, he received a letter from his sister, Filomena, telling him that their mother was dying. He requested leave to visit his mother, but he was denied permission to go. He was determined to see her and began striking out on his own, heading toward Marseilles where he hoped to get a ship to Sicily. He was apprehended before he arrived in Marseilles, however, and was sent to the stockade for being absent without leave. After a short time in the army jail, he went back to the front. He told us that he always regretted not seeing his mother before she died, but he never talked about his father.

Although he was wounded three times, as soon as the wounds healed he was always sent back to the front. His division slowly crossed France, reaching the eastern town of Nancy. However, he must have been able to enter Germany where he visited the famous Cologne Cathedral. It had made a strong impression on him when he could see imprints of bullet holes on the façade. There he purchased a pocket knife engraved with a picture of the cathedral, the only memento he cherished from the war.

After the war when he returned to Syracuse he bought a motorcycle. He had never driven one, and when he took his first ride he did not know how to stop it or turn off the engine. He rode it for hours until it ran out of gas. This was one of the stories Salvatore told us about our reckless Dad.

When each child was born, Daddy took them to visit Salvatore, who always brought out the best wine. Together, they would celebrate the new baby the way it was done in Sicily, drinking toasts to each other and to the baby.

Over an eleven year period, Almerinda and Frank produced four daughters and three sons. Their youngest child, Vincent, was born eleven years after Francis bringing the family to eight children. Daddy still believed that Italian families should have many children, and he was very proud of his brood. He believed that his children were gifts from God and that God would provide what was needed for him to support his family.

CHAPTER NINE

ANSWERED PRAYERS

One day in October upon returning from school, Mother Wells greeted me at the door.

"I have good news for you, your Dad is coming in a little while. You are going home!"

"Home? I'm going home?" I was almost speechless but managed to ask, "And what about my sisters?"

"The social worker told me your mother has been released from the hospital and you and Rosalie can go home. Charlotte and Doris can't join you yet. It might be too difficult for your mother to have all of her children at home at once. The four oldest ones will be the first to go and the younger ones will join your family later after your mother has adjusted to caring for you, Rosalie, and your brothers."

I had been praying for months for Mom to be released from the State Hospital so we could all be a family again. After living at Elmcrest for two years, my prayers were being answered, but suddenly I wasn't sure that going back was what I wanted after all. I didn't know what to expect at home. Based on what life was like before Mom went into the hospital, it was easy to assume that as the oldest I would have the responsibility of helping her adjust to being a homemaker again. I was a little worried about how much responsibility that would be. I also worried that going home might mean we would have to change schools.

I didn't want to leave Doris and Charlotte behind and I knew it would be hard to leave my best friend, Helen. I desperately wanted stay at Nottingham High School, where we could continue to see each other. Our walk to school together was one of the best parts of my day.

I tried to look on the bright side. At least we could take our clothes with us, and we'd still attend the same church, Park Central, where we would meet Doris, Charlotte, and our youngest brother, Fran. I assumed they would come home with us for the Sunday meal. So, with both excitement and misgivings, Rosalie and I gathered our clothes, school books, and music to be ready to leave when Dad arrived. There was no time to say good-bye to Helen.

Soon Dad arrived in the Mondo truck to pick up the four of us—Rosalie and me and my brothers. He had a broad grin, so happy to be reuniting his family.

As we piled into the truck, he turned to me and said, "You see, our prayers have been answered."

When we arrived home, Mom looked the same as she had before going to the hospital. She was in the kitchen wearing her familiar house dress, with a smile on her face as she stirred the soup. She looked happy and spoke softly, "How I missed you!" She held out her arms to hug and kiss each of us. As she turned back to the stove everything seemed so normal, as if no time had passed and nothing had changed. Rosalie and I set the table, and Mom said it was Ronnie and David's turn to wash dishes after supper.

At supper, things were the same too: Daddy encouraged us to "*Mangia con pane!*" —eat with bread—urging us to fill up our stomachs with bread, since the broth had no meat or vegetables in it, and soup was all we had.

Mom, however, was different in surprising ways. While we were eating, she spoke of wanting to finish high school. At the age of thirty-three, she was awakening to new possibilities for herself. She said she intended to enroll in an evening program. The next day she registered, and two nights later began taking a literature class. Every day she would read for hours, and from the look on her face I could see she was lost in the stories. One afternoon when I returned from school she was so caught up in feeling sorry for Hester Pryne, of the *Scarlet Letter* she had forgotten to start supper. To protect her from the anger I knew my father would direct at her, I prepared supper for the family.

Mom loved getting away from the house to go to school. "It's wonderful to feel so free to do what I have always wanted to do

—go to school. After I get my high school diploma, I want to go to nursing school," she told me.

In the meantime, I had been contemplating how I could stay at Nottingham High School. I told Mom I didn't want to go to North High, which was close to where we lived. I'd made good friends at Nottingham and wanted to continue there. She shook her head, as if to say "impossible." "You know the rules. You have to go to the school closest to where you live."

Rosalie, David, and Ronnie registered in their old schools but I wanted to remain at my high school where I was a sophomore. I pressed my case, "Mom, I really don't want to lose my friends and I'm a leader in Y-teens at Nottingham."

Mom listened to me and seemed to understand my need to stay in the school where I had friends. I said, "Mom, what if we asked the superintendent of schools for permission for me to continue at Nottingham? We could say that I want to take German and it is not offered at North High, only at Nottingham. Would you make a special request to the school superintendent for me?"

Mom agreed and the two of us met with the superintendent. Just as we rehearsed, she explained that I wanted to take German and the high school near our home did not offer it. The superintendent said that was reasonable and granted our request. As he walked us to the door he said, "I wish all the problems I have to solve were as easy as this one."

Once outside his office, I hugged Mom. I was ecstatic, and thanked her profusely. She hugged me back but said, "You know this means you will have to be up and out of the house before seven each morning and take two buses across town to be on time for school."

"I will, I promise."

It was so important for me to continue at Nottingham that I had no difficulty getting up and leaving home so early. Each day at school I enjoyed seeing my friends, Jean and Joan, the twins, Ann one of my friends from church, and I especially looked forward to seeing Helen when I arrived each morning. She always asked how my mother was doing and I reluctantly told her that life at home was not as I'd hoped.

"My Mom's having trouble adjusting to having the four of us at home."

Helen asked, "But isn't it wonderful she's so interested in school?"

"I'm glad she is going to night school, but it's difficult for her to keep up with the chores: washing, ironing, cleaning and cooking."

Helen said, "But it must be tough for her trying to keep up with her homework and keep house for all six of you, too."

Dad was opposed to Mom going to school, because the classes were at night and she'd be out alone. He worried that she might wander away and get lost. We four kids and Dad would lie in our beds wide awake until we heard her key in the lock, sometimes as late as eleven o'clock. He also complained she would not be able to do her 'job' at home, but she insisted the meals would be prepared on time and the chores would be done before she went to class.

Three nights a week she had class. She usually hadn't prepared the evening meal yet, but no matter what Dad said, she picked up her books and left. It was not long before Dad began scolding Mom. Then he turned on me, "You should help you mother, you don' wan' her go back to hospital, do you?"

I took over when my mother didn't complete her tasks, but was confused about who was in charge. Some days it felt as if my mother and I were in a tug of war. She was the mother, and was supposed to take care of us, but when I returned from school it was obvious that she hadn't completed the housework. Yet when Rosalie and I pitched in to help her, she would say, "No, that's my job." When I saw her frown and look down I knew she was upset. She often said, "I can do that tomorrow." We were used to having our clothes and sheets washed on Mondays but week after week, the laundry piled up for the six of us.

Not wanting to hurt her feelings, I would gently insist that the washing needed to be done now, because we needed clean clothes for the next day. But most nights her response was the same: "I never got around to... washing clothes, or cleaning, or cooking supper. I was too busy getting ready for class tonight."

When Daddy bought our first Easy Spin washing machine, Rosalie and I thought that would help Mom get the clothes washed on time. It meant that the clothes could be spun to extract as much water as possible before they were hung to dry. Until the spin dryer, each piece of clothing had to be pressed through ringers by hand, a time-consuming ordeal. The new spin dryer was not like the electric dryers of today, but it did help the clothes dry more quickly. But before long, we realized that the new washing machine was not enough of an incentive to help Mom get the laundry done.

I began doing the wash by dragging the washer away from the wall where it was stored, connecting it to the kitchen sink, sorting the clothes, and washing them load by load. It was inconvenient trying to prepare supper at the same time the sink was being used for draining the washer between loads, but if we waited until after supper, we couldn't get it all done. We did our best to get most of the clothes washed and hung in the cold cellar, knowing they wouldn't be dry by morning. Sometimes Rosalie and I would iron some of the wet clothes so they'd be dry enough to wear, they remained damp.

We had trouble getting our own homework done because we were doing much of the housework. I began to resent not having time to practice the piano. Every night, in addition to laundry chores and making dinner, there were lunches to prepare for the next day. I tried to do it all, but finally I complained to Daddy. He replied in his usual way: "You don' wan' you mother go back to hospital, do you?" My answer was always, "Of course not."

Most of the time I felt she was acting more like a child, when she was supposed to be the adult. I was taking care of my mother, my sister and brothers and I became more and more resentful.

One day I returned home to find Mom preparing soup again. We seemed to be having soup almost every night. At least this time it was minestrone. She asked me to cut up some carrots and celery for the soup and bring up a jar of tomato sauce from the cellar. I said I did not have time and went to the piano to practice, but Mom yelled for me to return to the kitchen to help her. I told her I needed to practice, and mouthed off, "Why can't you cut up the vegetables?"

The next thing I knew she hauled off and slapped me. My cheek was burning. What a shock! She had never slapped me before. I began to cry, more from rage and hurt feelings than actual pain. I was humiliated and furious and left the kitchen wiping away my tears. How could she, when I was always the one who helped her? I went to the bedroom where I could be alone and sulk.

About half an hour later Rosalie came in, and in an agitated state told me Mom had lost her wedding ring in the pot of soup. "We need you to help us strain the big pot, it's full of chicken bones and vegetables. Mom thinks the ring may be hiding somewhere in the bottom of the pot."

At last we found it, and we three agreed not to tell Dad about what happened. It appeared that everyone else had forgotten the slap and my humiliation but I hadn't.

Most of the time my mother and all of us children managed to have fun despite our poverty and Dad's iron hand. David and Ronnie found a way to earn some spending money at the German luncheon club across from our house where the men gave the boys a nickel or dime for opening doors. Mom felt the boys were taking advantage of the men. She tried to stop them, but they were desperate to earn some spare change.

With their money and a few coins Mom saved from the food allowance, David, Ronnie, Rosalie and I walked a mile to MacArthur Stadium to watch our favorite baseball team, the Syracuse Chiefs. The Syracuse team was part of the minor leagues, the farm club for the New York Yankee major league team. When there was not enough money, David and Ronnie assured us they knew a way to sneak into the stadium. We found seats together in the bleachers to cheer our favorites: Hank Sauer, Clyde Vollmer, and Dutch Mele. We deferred to David's opinion about baseball asking him if he thought Hank Sauer would be sent to the Yankees. He always seemed to know about the team, and assured us that Hank wouldn't go to the Yankees until later in the season when someone on the Yankees team would need to be replaced.

We loved going to the baseball games. Mom would remind us not to tell Dad or he'd demand to know where we got the money, and there would be trouble. She also sneaked the boys out of the house to a movie on some Saturday afternoons. Rosalie and I would go to our piano lessons and Mom had the afternoon free. We could count on her to fix a special dessert for supper on those days.

This routine went on for about three months. One day we were surprised and shocked when the ambulance from Marcy State hospital and men in white coats arrived to take Mom back to the hospital. Dad was still at work, and we had just returned from school. We endured a wrenching scene with the neighbors gawking as Mom screamed and kicked, trying to get away from the men who were restraining her.

David and Ronnie pulled on their sleeves, yelling, "Stop, Stop! You're hurting our mother, stop!" But they were helpless to prevent the men from taking her.

After the ambulance pulled away, we closed the doors and windows to hide from our neighbors. We were embarrassed at the scene they had witnessed and terribly upset that we could not protect our mother. All of us were burning with guilt and shame that our mother had been dragged away in a straight jacket. Now the neighbors would know she was not going to the local hospital, that she was crazy.

We did not know what to do or whom to contact. We were alone in the house, without a phone. All we could do was huddle together in the living room and wait for Dad to return from work. Distraught, David and Ronnie asked, "Will we have to go back to Elmcrest?"

Rosalie and I hung our heads. I answered, "Yes, probably we'll all have to go back."

It never occurred to us to ask who might have called the hospital or why they came to get her. Perhaps, Dad had inadvertently set it in motion when the doctor would ask him how my mother was doing.

Sure enough, the next day Daddy returned us to Elmcrest. Oddly, as I walked in the door, I felt safe again, like I'd come home. We returned to the familiar routine: going to school with friends, taking care of our chores, having regular meals, and doing our homework. Both Rosalie and I were glad that we could practice the piano again without interruptions.

The next year Mom was released again and the four of us: David, Ronnie, Rosalie and I returned home. We kids felt conflicted. We wanted our family to be together, but changing schools so often was difficult for my brothers and Rosalie. The boys had trouble making friends and keeping them, and they couldn't keep up with their school work. I was not as affected in these ways because I didn't change schools.

Mother's release and return to the hospital became a recurring nightmare. Apparently the shock treatments didn't help her cope with the pressures of children, household tasks, and my father's demands. After a few months the state hospital ambulance would arrive again and our mother would be hauled away, leaving us feeling confused, helpless, and ashamed once more.

After my mother returned to the hospital for the third time, a social worker summoned Daddy to a meeting at Marcy State Hospital. He asked me to come along and help explain the complexities of medical treatment. I was used to translating for him in this way and wasn't alarmed at the prospect.

But what the social worker told us was very upsetting. The electric shock treatments had not worked, she said, but there was a new method for treating Mom's condition that the doctors thought would help. They wanted to perform a surgery called a lobotomy, and they needed Dad's written permission.

The woman explained how a lobotomy was performed. "The surgeon will make a small cut that will sever the frontal lobe of the brain." She said, pointing to the front of her head. "There is a fifty-fifty chance that it will work. It has helped some people return to a normal or near-normal life."

Dad looked troubled and shook his head, "I don' understand how this can help her."

The social worker explained, "The surgery can make your wife less agitated and unhappy. We cannot guarantee that the surgery will be successful but we have nothing else to offer you."

Dad asked, "Isn't there any medicine you can give her?"

She shook her head, "Not at the present time. Perhaps in a few years there may be some drugs that might work, but there is nothing right now. I suggest you go home and think about this and let us know what you decide. Here is the consent form you will need to sign to give the doctors permission to perform this operation."

As we prepared to leave she said, "Thousands of these operations have been done in New York State, and about half of the patients were able to return to their homes "cured" of their mental illness. However, many patients need a great deal of looking after. Almost all the patients had some loss of memory, but for some their memory gradually returns."

I asked, "What does that mean—a great deal of looking after?"

The answer frightened me. "Your mother might not be able to think like an adult at first. She might have the decision-making ability of a three-year-old to begin with, but her mental capacity might increase over time. There are no guarantees, but we have nothing else to offer. She might end up being a patient here for the rest of her life. There are no alternatives and no guarantees."

I was quiet as I pondered what it would be like to have my mother making decisions like a three-year-old. I thought about how Charlotte and Fran had acted when they were three. We could not trust them to be out of the house alone. What would that mean for my mother, and for me if I were expected to look after her?

On the way back to Syracuse, Daddy said we needed to pray about this, and in a few weeks we would decide what to do. At sixteen, I felt totally inadequate to help Dad make such an important decision. I discussed it with Aunt Fay, but she said she did not know enough to advise us. Of course, I prayed hard that Dad would make the right decision.

After a couple of weeks he announced, "We should give permission to the hospital to do this operation. It might help her, and then she could come home for good."

I returned to my normal life at Elmcrest and waited for Dad to tell me when Mom had had the surgery, continuing to pray for her healing. About three months later Dad told me she'd had the surgery. He wanted to visit her, and asked me to go with him.

Mom seemed subdued, her spirit gone. She kept her head bowed, and her eyes only focused on the floor. She did not smile but said in a low voice, "I'm fine, I feel good, and I want to come home someday."

I was anxious to see if she had lost some of her beautiful wavy hair. I assumed some had fallen out but she looked the same.

This time when we left, there was no screaming, yelling, or begging us to help her. She did not plead for us to take her home. It was a pleasant visit for a change. Dad and I were relieved that she was complacent.

The nurse told us, "The doctors are pleased that she's made such a good adjustment to the hospital routine."

On the way back to Elmcrest, we discussed how much better it was to have her be so calm. Daddy didn't know when she could come home but was sure she would be released soon. He told me to keep praying.

After eight months in the hospital, the day finally arrived for

Mom to come home. It was in the middle of the school year, which meant that Rosalie, David and Ronnie had to change schools again. This time we hoped she would stay home forever, but as the oldest, I was skeptical. I remembered how the social worker said she might not be able to remember much from before the lobotomy and that she would need a great deal of looking after, which turned out to be true.

My father relied on me to do a lot of things for him, such as filling out his income tax forms, and his union business. He would not accept that at sixteen I was not an adult by societal standards. Though my mother was at home, he gave me some money and asked me to go downtown and buy a set of bunk beds for David and Ronnie. They'd been sleeping on what was called a three-quarters bed, slightly larger than a twin bed. It had long since become too small for the growing boys who were eleven and twelve years old.

Both the salesman and the manager refused the money I offered, saying that I was not old enough to make such a purchase. I assured them we would make weekly payments and would not expect delivery until the beds were fully paid. The two men would not hear of doing business with me. I returned home, handed the money back to my father and reported what had occurred. He was furious. All the stores closed at five-thirty each evening meaning Dad would have to take time off from work to buy the beds himself. He did not trust Mom to purchase the beds as she was frequently wandering off.

He said, "Di'n't you show them the money I give you? Why di'n't you insist?" He could not accept that the men thought I was too young to do business. "How can I take off work? Why cou'n't you buy the beds?"

I was sorry I had disappointed him, but I felt I had done my best. There was no alternative but for him to leave work early to buy the beds.

After a few weeks time I returned from school to find the washing machine in the middle of the kitchen floor, the washing unfinished, my mother nowhere in sight. *Here we go again,* I thought. *We'll have to find her and clean up this mess.* It was logical that Rosalie and I would take care of the laundry while the boys looked for Mom. Daddy would not be home for a couple of hours, and naturally we didn't want him to know about this.

We all tried to figure out where she'd gone. I suggested, "First try Grandma's. If she is not there, look downtown."

The boys headed out on their mission while Rosalie and I finished the washing. We prepared supper, too, trying not to be upset that the same thing was happening all over again. Since there was a light rain, we hung the wet clothes in the cellar and draped some of the clothes near the radiators. Of course, we worried about Mom. Where was she? Was she all right? As usual, there was no time for homework or practicing that night.

After a couple of hours, the boys came back with Mom. They told us that they had found her coming out of Woolworth's. To our relief she had not been shoplifting, one of the things I had worried about. Apparently, Mom had been wandering in and out of the stores downtown, lost in her own thoughts. I asked, "Mom, where were you? We were worried when we came home from school and you weren't here."

"I just went for a walk, nothing to worry about," she said.

This became a familiar pattern: she would begin supper and then disappear, leaving me to finish the job. Fortunately, she always turned off the burners on the stove before she went wandering.

Sometimes the boys would find her coming out of a movie theater. They said she always seemed glad to see them and told them about the movie as they escorted her home.

When I finally told Dad that Mom had been disappearing, he scolded me, "You have to take care of her or she will have to go back to Marcy and you all go back to Elmcrest. Is that what you want?"

Of course, I did not want her to return to the hospital, but I felt both resentful and frustrated. I was not even home from school when she wandered off, so what could I do? I wondered if Dad wanted me to quit school to take care of our mother, but I didn't want to ask him for fear he would say yes.

On the days when Mom was not wandering around Syracuse, we would find her happily preparing a snack for us after school and singing some of the popular songs of the day. "Paper Moon," "I'll Get By," "The White Cliffs of Dover," all the songs related to the war and young men leaving their sweethearts behind. When Daddy heard her singing these songs he would chastise her in Italian, saying they were not appropriate for us kids. That's when she began singing hymns. "What A Friend We Have in Jesus," and the "The Old Rugged Cross" these hymns were favorites of Dad's, too. If she persuaded him to sing with her, he'd always be in a better mood. They both had beautiful voices. They loved to sing and we loved listening to them.

On such days we were happy to be home, and we hoped Doris, Charlotte, and Fran would be able to come home soon. However, after eight months of these episodes of Mom leaving the house with no supper prepared and chores undone, it was obvious she could not cope.

During this period, I was grateful for choir rehearsal every Thursday evening and the Sunday youth group where I could escape the chaos at home. It was such a relief to sing, and I almost never missed a rehearsal. I always felt exhilarated after singing. Sometimes on Sunday evenings someone in the youth group would give me a ride home and ask how things were going. I'd claim it was good to be home and to be with my mother again. I said what everyone wanted to hear, not letting on that things were not perfect. My music and my church had become the haven that my home could never be.

What turned out to be the final time our mother was taken away, we were not surprised to see the ambulance arrive, but it was still very upsetting to the four of us to stand by helplessly watching the men tie her arms and lift her into the state hospital's ambulance like a sack of potatoes. She did not resist and yell as much as previous times. Perhaps she knew that she had to return to the hospital, and maybe she felt okay about it. As before, we still could not protect her or ourselves from the prying eyes of all the neighbors. Some of the neighbor kids yelled, "They're taking the crazy lady back to the hospital." We never got used to the neighbors' reactions and tried to hide from their stares and judgements. It felt so hurtful to hear our mother described as crazy.

We watched the ambulance leave, then the four of us huddled on the living room sofa, Ronnie crying, the rest of us morose but trying to hide our tears. Our hope of living like a normal family had evaporated again and we had come to believe that our prayers would never be answered.

The last few months at home had been Mom's last chance to return to a normal life, and it didn't work out. Of course, I blamed myself. I should have done more to help her cope. Now we knew we had to go back to Elmcrest.

I felt wretched with guilt, but the truth was that life was easier for all of us at Elmcrest. We had a familiar routine, meals were prepared for us, we did our homework, we had friends, and Rosalie and I could practice the piano again.

At times I felt perhaps if I had been less resentful I might have been more helpful to my mother but I was still a teenager and should not have been expected to carry so much responsibility. In spite of everyone expecting me to be an adult, there was much I did not know about caring for a person with mental illness and I felt quite unprepared to play the role of "little mother." I wonder if the hospital social worker could have better prepared us for the return of a mother who had had a lobotomy.

CHAPTER TEN

SPIRITUALITY

One night when I was about nine years old my mother and Aunt Fay took me to the big Baptist Church in downtown Syracuse to hear Billy Graham. He was a young minister they called an evangelist who was traveling the country to preach, and Mom and Aunt Fay wanted to hear him. Aunt Fay told me that another evangelist named Billy Sunday was the one who had first inspired my grandfather when he had come to this country. She said she thought Billy Graham was similar to Billy Sunday.

I found it exciting singing hymns sitting between my mom and my aunt. We sang the same tunes at my parents' church but here the words were in English. Everyone sang loudly and passionately before Billy Graham began to preach. He was very down to earth, and I could understand everything he was saying. He urged us to give our lives to Christ Jesus, saying that was the only way to be saved from sin. At the end of his sermon he invited people to come forward to dedicate their lives to Christ. At Billy Graham's urging many people went down to the front of the church to be "saved" and to change their lives. I expected that we three would join the others but my mother and Aunt Fay did not join the large numbers of people who did. Mom said we would have to leave because it was a school night and I had to get my sleep. As we began to leave, Mom said she was feeling sick and she was hemorrhaging. Aunt Fay called a taxi. I was worried and asked Mom if she should go to the hospital but as I helped her into the cab she said, "Don't worry, I'll be alright." She told me later that she had lost the baby. I didn't know she was expecting another baby but she did not seem to be upset. I had hoped that we could have gone another night to hear Billy Graham again but Mom said she had to rest. I had such mixed feelings. I was excited about going out on a school night with my mother and Aunt Fay, inspired by the young Billy Graham and joyfully singing with so many people and, at the same time worrying about my mother's health. I wondered if she really would be all right. For the next few days I looked after her until she told me she felt fine.

Billy Graham had made an impression on me and I wanted to feel that I belonged to Christ Jesus to receive salvation even though I did not really know what that meant. I knew it had something to do with trusting God to lead me. It was the first time I was aware of spiritual yearnings.

My experience of worship at the orphanage had been a far cry from that night with Billy Graham. But it got better when Mr. Joiner fulfilled his promise to do something about Sunday worship at Elmcrest, and we began going to one of the downtown churches. Each Sunday the seven Messinas along with my best friend Helen and several other children, boarded the bus for church. I looked forward to it because I was warmly welcomed and was beginning to make friends with my new classmates in Sunday School.

Though worship at Park Central was nothing like Billy Graham, I really liked the friendly way everyone at the church greeted us, it made me feel comfortable and at home.

Mr. Mielke, the minister of Park Central, was in his early thirties. Some people thought he was too young to be the senior minister of such a large church, but after worship each Sunday many people greeted Mr. Mielke and told him they appreciated his sermon. I began to be aware that he was an excellent preacher —he did not talk down to the congregation and it was easy to follow his sermons. Sometimes Helen and I discussed them and we both liked the way he related the Bible to our everyday lives.

Over time I developed a close relationship to all the church staff. Mrs. McCorkle was the Director of Christian Education, whose job it was to recruit and train teachers for the Sunday School. A war widow with two young children, she had to work full time. Sometimes she would ask me to play the hymns for a special worship service. When there was a pot luck supper at church, she always invited me. "Jerry, you do not need to bring anything, I've made a large enough casserole for you to join our family at the potluck." I loved feeling included in the church's activities, and being welcomed by Mrs. McCorkle.

Several others in the church took me under their wings. A young couple, Charlene and Fred, became advisors for the senior high group that Helen and I attended, and Mr. Carruth, a young man in his twenties, was the organist and choir director. Mrs. McCorkle told me everyone was very pleased when he joined the church staff, he had a reputation as an outstanding musician. Because of my interest in music, I got to know him quite well, and he inspired me when he played Bach before church each Sunday. During the summer programs, I was pleased when he asked me to play the piano and lead the singing for the grade school classes.

Although Mr. Mielke, the minister, was a tall, stern-looking man with a serious expression on his face, I came to know him as a compassionate teacher through the eight-week confirmation class to prepare us for church membership. He guided us in exploring the Bible, and explained the origins of the presbyterian church. We learned what membership would mean for us. I was eager to learn, asking questions about history and presbyterian beliefs.

Mr. Mielke asked us to memorize a Psalm along with some hymns he thought would have special meaning for us. One hymn I loved—*Joyful, Joyful, We Adore Thee*—was from a familiar Beethoven theme. Although my classmates complained about having to memorize a Psalm, I was inspired by the eighth Psalm, which speaks of God's glory in the firmament and the earth. Mr. Mielke recognized I was deeply moved by it when I recited it in class.

The Psalm reminded me of a time when Daddy took me out to look at the night sky, pointing out the Milky Way, the Big Dipper, and other constellations. My sisters, brothers, and I had marveled that Dad, who only had a third grade education, knew how to read the stars. When Daddy expressed amazement at what God had created, I, too, felt that same awe.

As we studied the Eighth Psalm, I pictured the psalmist gazing at the moon and the stars with a sense of wonder similar to my Dad's. Mr. Mielke invited me to recite it in front of the whole congregation one Sunday morning. At first I declined, terrified at the thought of getting up in front of so many people. There were usually about eight hundred at the Sunday morning services. Thanks to his encouragement, I agreed. Although I was too shy to give an oral book report at school, I did not feel as timid at church with Mr. Mielke's presence. When the time arrived, I walked up the steps of the chancel, all eyes on me. I calmed myself by remembering what it was like to look at the night sky, and pretended to be the Psalmist.

O Lord, our Lord, How excellent is thy name in all the earth.
When I consider thy heavens, the work of thy fingers
The moon and the stars, which thou has ordained;
What is man and woman, that thou are mindful of us?
And the son of man, that thou visitest us?
For thou has made us a little lower than the angels
And has crowned us with glory and honor...
Thou has put all things under our feet: all sheep and oxen, yea
And the beasts of the field, the fowl of the air, and the fish of the sea,
O Lord, our Lord how excellent is thy name in all the earth!

I held the psalm close to my heart. It reminded me that God was in charge. Each morning while I was still in bed at the orphanage, I would begin my prayers with the first verse, *"O Lord, my Lord, How excellent is your name in all the earth!"* Sometimes while I was brushing my teeth the words of the psalm came to my mind and I would feel the weight of my burdens begin to lift. I realized I could stop worrying about my mother. God would take care of her. God was holding things in place in my universe. This understanding released me from feeling that I alone was responsible for my family.

Every day when Helen and I walked to school we would talk about everything —school, church, new ideas. As girls, it meant a lot to us to feel included when Mr. Mielke told us we could add the word "woman" wherever "man" appeared in the Bible. He said, "The Bible was written by men at a time when girls and women were not educated. But today we know that God's Word is for both women and men." Helen said, "It's exciting to know that we girls are not to be left out."

I agreed with her, adding, "It's a new idea I expect my father won't approve of. My Dad believes every word in the Bible comes directly from God. I'm sure he'll disagree with Mr. Mielke and not accept the addition of any word, especially one that implies the equality of women with men." I really liked what I was learning and wished I could discuss it with my mother. I thought she would like this new idea, too.

Helen said she wondered why it was such a problem for people to accept that God would want to include women. It seemed so obvious that a just God would treat us the same as men.

We were learning in our confirmation class that many authors wrote the books of the Bible, and that the psalms were probably written by many people, not only King David. I knew I would never be able to convince my father of the new things I was learning.

I was particularly interested in church history: Presbyterian beliefs, how the church came into being, and the role of John Calvin and John Knox laying the foundation for the Presbyterian Church. I drank it all in. I had difficulty understanding Calvin's predestination theology which Mr. Mielke said many people misunderstood. He reassured us that God was not manipulating us humans like puppets on a string. He said we had the freedom to choose our own path with God's help if we asked. God's unearned favor or "grace" given to us can then be extended "graciously" by us to others. I liked what I was learning, to know there was so much freedom and wanted to learn more. I could plan my own future and I had choices, but as a Christian I could ask for God's guidance. I became more convinced that I belonged at Park Central Presbyterian Church with my new adult friends on the staff, as well as the friends who were my age: Helen, Barbara, and Anne, Buster, and Dave. It was clear to me that this church along with all my friends would be my spiritual home.

As we learned about what rituals were required for admittance, to my relief I found out that baptism did not require dunking as I'd seen in my parents' church, but just a sprinkling of water by the minister. It was a gesture that symbolized being dunked into water as Jesus had been. I had always hoped I could avoid being dipped into the pool in my parents' church, afraid the minister might let go of me. That was no longer a worry for me, since my baptism would be a sprinkle of water on my head.

As the day approached for our confirmation, the whole class talked about what we would wear and how we looked forward to having our families there. Before the confirmation ceremony, I would be the only one who would be baptized since all the others had been baptized as infants. My parents would not be there, but all of my sisters and brothers would be sitting near the front of the church.

Keeping my head bowed I felt the water trickle onto my head, I prayed silently to be worthy of being called a follower of Christ. Then all twelve of us from the confirmation class took the vows that confirmed our commitment to church membership. Mr. Mielke said prayers that all of us would follow the teachings of Jesus and that God would protect us from harm.

What a solemn and happy moment! The elders of the church came forward, congratulating me for making the decision to be baptized and welcomed all of us into the membership by shaking our hands. I felt very grown up and proud because I'd had the courage to be baptized, and had made the decision on my own to join the presbyterian church without consulting my father. I hoped that my sisters and brothers would follow my lead. Many people in the congregation also came up to shake my hand and welcome me. My sisters and brothers came forward and hugged me. Rosalie said she wanted to be baptized when she was eligible to attend the confirmation class. I felt more secure belonging to Park Central Church. It was a new experience for me having a sense of security.

I knew there would be a battle with Dad when I told him I was baptized and had joined the presbyterian church. I dreaded the inevitable confrontation with him. As I expected, when I arrived for Sunday dinner and told him the news, Dad railed, "That kind of baptism is the catholic way! It should not be that way! What kind of baptism is that, sprinkling water on your head? You should be baptized in the pool in our church."

"It means the same as dunking the whole body, it's a symbol of the way Jesus was baptized. The presbyterian church is protestant, not catholic. How could we get to your church in Solvay? It's too far away. The buses take all of us from Elmcrest to the downtown churches, they won't take us all the way to Solvay."

Disagreeing, he shook his head, but I continued to try to

reassure him, "We all go to Sunday School each week, we are learning about the Bible. The minister at the church is helping us, even getting us scholarships to go to church camps this summer. Daddy, you don't have to worry, we are not going to be catholics."

It was hard for him to adjust to so many changes. First, he had lost his wife to the state hospital, then his children to the orphanage, and now we were lost to his much loved Italian protestant church.

He said, "*Meno malo*, at least you go to church." He appeared resigned to what was happening to his family.

He continued, "Gialdina, (he had trouble saying Geraldine and for many years wouldn't call me Jerry, my preference) read and study your Bible, pray every day." We agreed that those practices were the important ones to a spiritual life.

I kept reassuring him, "We all study the Bible at Sunday School and we all say our prayers, especially for Mom to get well and return home."

But nothing I could say fully satisfied him. He went on, "Not just in Sunday School but during the week, too." For the next several months he kept urging more Bible study as if he couldn't trust that we were getting enough Bible in Sunday School.

Mrs. McCorkle, along with Fred and Charlene, our youth group advisors, gradually gave me more leadership responsibilities. They told me I had organizational skills and selected me to represent our church at city-wide interdenominational meetings as well as youth meetings at the Presbytery level (similar to the county level in government.) We called ourselves "CQ"—Comrades of the Quest. There were about twenty-five in our group and we met every Sunday evening for about two hours. Belonging to this group and attending meetings was the highlight of my week.

My self-confidence grew as I recognized my skill in explaining issues that others had difficulty understanding. I noticed that others turned to me to summarize discussions. One evening Charlene told me how much she appreciated my contributions, "When you say you will do something we know you will, we can always count on you. That's the mark of a good leader."

The more involved I became at church, the more my faith grew. I was aware that when my mother first went into the hospital and we first moved to the orphanage, I felt very lonely and fearful of what might be happening to us. I worried that our family might be broken up forever. Now the joy I experienced from music and my involvement with my youth group were erasing my sense of foreboding about life, bringing with it a feeling of serenity. My sisters and brothers gradually became involved in Park Central, giving me more confidence that our family was still "together."

I became reflective, feeling that God was leading me, although I was not sure where. I wondered about my purpose on earth. In my prayers I would ask God what He wanted me to do with my life. I was thankful to no longer feel burdened with family responsibilities and I didn't have to worry any more about food and clothes and taking care of my brothers and sisters. I had a sense of relief as those burdens were lifted from me.

My church school teacher, Mr. Rice, another one of my friends, was beginning to influence my thoughts about my future. Perhaps, he had seen my reactions when others in my church school class discussed going to college. Their parents expected them to attend college after high school, but there was no such expectation in my family. Mr. Rice presented me with college brochures, gradually strengthening my desire to go. He would say, "It is possible for you to go, and we here at the church will help you."

I believed that God had sent these special people into my life for a purpose. No one else had expressed any confidence in my ability to go to college. Words of my high school counselor echoed in my ear, to take typing, that maybe I could be a secretary after high school. In fact, she told me to forget about college.

Her words were so powerful that I was convinced I should not consider more schooling upon graduation. However, my church friends continued to tell me they wanted to help me with scholarships, knowing I did not have money for a college education. They were willing and able to show me a way. Their words of support made all the difference. I began to believe that it might be possible, and I was determined to plan for college.

As I became more tuned into my faith, I began to struggle with questions about my father. I sometimes wondered how my father could have such a strong faith, always studying the Bible, praying, and yet at times he beat my mother and us children. I remember reading the phrase, "We kill what we love." I did not understand it but it made me think of my father's violence. I knew my Dad was not intending to kill our spirits —perhaps it was his way to show how much he loved us. I wondered when he kneeled to pray by the side of his bed if he ever asked for forgiveness for beating Mom and, especially, my brothers. We made fun of him kneeling to pray, but we still admired him for taking his evening prayers so seriously. I felt I needed to find a way to forgive him for his actions, though he had not asked for it. I did not want to hate him, and yet there were times when I felt disgusted with him and disapproving of his old-world ways.

Even as young as nine years old, I had recognized that life was overwhelming for my father, that he did not always know how to deal with expectations this country placed upon him. Now that he was alone, I was the one he depended on to read and explain documents he could not understand. With his limited English, life often seemed a puzzle to him and he did not always know what to do. My feelings for my father swung back and forth: sympathy for his inability to cope with life in America and frustration with having to guide him through his ignorance. I could be so angry with him for the way he treated us, and sorry that he was now alone except when we joined him for Sunday dinners.

The youth group continued to give me the safe haven I needed—such a contrast to the turmoil at home.

For two years I was content to attend church on Sundays. Then one day Mr. Carruth, the choir director, invited Helen and me to sing in the senior choir, and Sundays became even more important. We both were surprised since we were still in high school and only adults attended the Senior Choir. We knew that four of the choir members were paid professional musicians, and the choir had a city-wide reputation of singing challenging music, even oratorios. Mr. Carruth told us he was impressed with how well we could sight read and that we had strong voices. What an exciting privilege to be good enough for the adult choir. We never missed the rehearsals on Thursday evenings, for we knew if we were not at rehearsal we would not be allowed to sing on Sunday.

Soon after joining the choir, Mrs. Sheard, the professional soprano, offered to give me free voice lessons. I was honored and thrilled. Each week for the next two years, I would take two buses to her house for lessons. She'd sit at her piano and teach me how to control my breathing and my voice and showed me how to use it in phrasing. She introduced me to arias from Italian and French operas. I learned how important it was to breathe from the diaphragm and not just from the chest, and how to develop the range and timbre of my voice. Thanks to Mrs. Sheard, my confidence was increasing as I learned to project my voice without feeling self-conscious. She would often say, "For such a little person, you have a big voice and you have a very wide range. With more training you definitely could be a coloratura, but at present you have the range of a lyric soprano, a beautiful voice."

At the time I did not realize that she was laying a foundation that later allowed me to sing solos and with some of the finest choral groups in this country and in Britain. I learned to enjoy the classical, operatic, and choral repertoire. I began to appreciate that I did have a beautiful voice, especially as I learned to breathe correctly and sing with feeling but without forcing the high notes.

When she first chose an Italian aria she was surprised that I was able to translate the words. She smiled approvingly. "So you know a little Italian. That will help you to know what you are singing about so you can sing with appropriate emotion."

One of my favorites was *Ombra Mai Fu* from Handel's opera *Xerxes*, because a favorite hymn tune had been adapted from it. I loved singing Giordani's *Caro Mio Ben* for the sad melodic line and Mrs. Sheard showed me how to reflect the loneliness in my singing by singing it two different ways. The English translation began:

Dearest, believe, when we must part, lonely I grieve, in my poor heart!
When we must part, sadly I grieve, in my lonely heart!

Mrs. Sheard would introduce the piece using words and melodies of these romantic operas, then she would show me how to sing not just words, but how to use my emotions, and create an authentic expression of what I was singing. She would demonstrate and I'd put into practice her teaching, showing her I understood. She taught me how to produce a mellow sound even when I sang the high notes. She showed me how to develop and extend my range. Thanks to her, my confidence continued to increase. Her compliments made me feel much taller than my five feet. At the end of my lesson, when we sang a duet together, it was pure joy to know that I had pleased her, for she clearly enjoyed singing with me. Each time I could tell how much better my voice sounded than when I had first arrived for my lesson. I always returned to Elmcrest exhilarated.

Each summer we attended camp and conferences, and there I experienced an intimacy with God that I had not had before. Perhaps enjoying nature—the green grass on the rolling hills, the giant trees surrounding the campus of Wells College where the conferences were held, and looking out on Cayuga Lake, one of the Finger Lakes in Central New York State—contributed to my feeling of closeness to God. From high up on a hill, we campers watched the impressive sunsets each night, awestricken. Our counselors referred to these as "mountaintop experiences."

Each evening several hundred of us teens gathered on the hillside lawn where we sang camp songs and hymns, and listened to inspiring talks that addressed our teenage experiences. Of course, we always prayed. Sometimes one of the leaders would play his guitar and lead the singing. During those times, I felt at one with everyone as if we had always been singing and praying together. The camaraderie of all the kids harmonizing gave me a tremendous sense of the power of music. The beauty of the lake at sunset contributed to it being truly the inspiring experience our counselors had told us was possible.

My music and religious encounters at church, at camp and conferences, contributed to a growing sense of spirituality which was sustaining me through the ups and downs of my adolescent years. I felt God's presence in my life. There was no dramatic moment or vision, as some people have experienced, but a steady awareness of God leading me. I was beginning to see my friends at church as angels guiding and encouraging me to go to college. I believed God was working through these angels to show me the way.

Mrs. McCorkle told me that many churches were looking for professionally trained Directors of Christian Education. She said it would be a way to combine my faith, my music, and my love of the church. She said I would need to not only have a college degree but would have to attend seminary. I thought seminaries were only for training ministers, but she told me that many seminaries had two-year programs to prepare students for a new profession called Christian Education. With this information, I began to think more seriously about my future.

CHAPTER ELEVEN

MOVING ON

*D*uring Nottingham's graduation I wore my cap and gown proudly. I was the first in my family to do so, but I had mixed feelings. I had met all the requirements for graduation, and though I had a good grade average, I was still unclear about whether I'd be able to go on to college like so many of my classmates.

After the exercises, all the graduates were looking for their parents and I looked for my father and Aunt Fay who had assured me they would be present. When we found each other, Dad hugged me and with a broad grin on his face handed me a gift.

"Is for you." I was surprised since I had not expected anything from him.

I opened the box, "Wow, a wrist watch! It's beautiful, I love it. Thank you, Daddy." I gave him another hug. He said, "You Aunt Fay picked it out."

Aunt Fay was standing by waiting for a hug from me.

"I really like it, Aunt Fay, you have very good taste. Thank you." I put my arms around her and kissed her on her soft cheek. She told me, "When I graduated from high school no one received expensive gifts like a watch. I am really proud that you have graduated, you are such a good example for your brothers and sisters.

I did not tell her that some of my classmates were anticipating a new car. I was pleased with my new watch. It meant that my father was proud of my accomplishment even though he could not put his thoughts into words. Later, I proudly showed off my watch to my sisters, brothers, and friends at Elmcrest.

The celebration of my graduation was short-lived. The next day I was scheduled to move out of Elmcrest. The rules required us to only remain at Elmcrest until we finished high school. I didn't want to leave, because I knew that living at home alone with my father would mean I'd be keeping house for him, something I was not looking forward to doing. I knew the rules, and had been anticipating that day. I gathered up my clothes, music, and other belongings and reluctantly said good-bye to Mother and Daddy Wells, who had also been encouraging me to go to college.

I hugged my three sisters, Helen, and many of the other girls, and assured them I would still visit them. I had such mixed feelings about leaving Elmcrest for the last time. It had been a safe, well-managed, and comfortable home for most of the last six years. I was not eager to go home for good. I anticipated many quarrels with Dad about my desire to go to college.

Immediately after graduation and with the help of one of the church elders, I was hired by Western Union as a switching clerk. Syracuse was the office where all messages for New York State (except for New York City) arrived and were electronically switched to the appropriate town. My love of geography helped me quickly learn where to send the messages. I began working to save for school. It would take more than a year to have enough money. There were times when it was exhausting, standing in one spot for eight hours. However, I kept my eyes on my goal to make as much money as possible for my first year of college. Sometimes I worked a double shift, sixteen hours, to earn the maximum amount of overtime pay. The efficiency manager at the company told my boss I was not only the fastest switching clerk he had encountered, but I was very efficient, wasting no movements in my work. Often Mr. G, my boss, would pull me away from my station to clear up another station where messages had piled up. He appreciated my speed in getting those messages to the intended receiver. He kept reminding the three of us clerks that speed and accuracy were Western Union's motto. Although saving money was my goal, I had learned the importance of working hard, and I soon developed a reputation as the one person Mr. G could count on most.

Several people at church, especially Mrs. McCorkle, warned me that some young people who had tried to work after high school to earn money for college would give up their plans when they began to enjoy spending their money. I was determined not to get trapped. I made regular deposits to my bank account as soon as I was paid, and carried my lunch to avoid additional expenses.

As expected, I couldn't escape the arguments with my father about my plans. Even my grandmother thought it was not necessary for girls to be educated beyond high school. At least Aunt Fay supported me. Although she did not have any money to contribute to my college account, she told me how much she admired how hard I was working. She told me she knew I was on the right track and she was praying for me. She would say, "With God's help, all things are possible."

I decided to ask some friends from church to help me convince my Dad. Sadie and Bob Kirk were in their sixties, and childless. They were attractive, white-haired, and gentle with each other. When I had a day off from work, I enjoyed going to their house for lunch and chatting with them in their garden, hearing stories of what it was like for them growing up in Scotland and the struggles they'd had coming to America. When I heard Sadie call Bob "Laddie," I would smile admiring their expression of genuine love and respect for each other.

Sadie and Bob were pleased when I asked them to come to meet my father. When they arrived, I welcomed them and made us some tea. At first, my father was cordial, asking them to sit at the dining room table.

Bob smiled and told Dad, "We are very fond of your daughter, and our church wants to help her to go to college. We know that money is tight for you, but Park Central Church can help with scholarships. There's a presbyterian college in Wooster, Ohio that is interested in her, and they will help her find work. She is smart and works hard. We believe in her."

My father began yelling at me in Italian, too upset to use English. "We have no money for college, it takes a lot of money, you know that! Why can't you be a secretary like Aunt Fay or a piano teacher? If you help me, all the kids can come home for good."

I answered in English that I did not want to be a secretary or a piano teacher but wanted to go to college and then seminary. He asked, "What's seminary?"

Bob Kirk explained, "Our church recognizes that Jerry feels called by God to serve the church as a Director of Christian

Education. The elders at our church examined her application, and we are convinced that she is sincere in her desire. We have decided to give her a scholarship. The first step is four years of college and then two years of seminary. It's the same place where ministers are trained."

My father turned toward me, ignoring the Kirks, "Why can't you help me so the kids can come home?" His voice rising, he went on, "You mean you been planning this for a long time and you di'n't tell me?"

"I was afraid to tell you, Daddy, because I knew you would get upset, just like you are now."

The Kirks said it was late and time for them to go home. I saw them to the door, reluctant for them to leave. I was grateful they had come, but now I would have to deal with my father alone. I dreaded the argument that I expected would continue, but finally we stopped talking and went to our respective bedrooms.

There were times when I felt guilty for causing dissension, but I was determined not to let him make me give up my dream of continuing my education. I saw college as a way out of a life of poverty. I did not want to be living as my father did from paycheck to paycheck, with little money for food and relying on the welfare department to provide some of the necessities for our family. For several months this wrangling continued, until reluctantly, he resigned himself to my decision.

Some days, when I thought of my brothers and sisters still living at Elmcrest, I wondered if I should give in to Dad's wishes and give up my desire for college. If I did, they could come home. I leaned heavily on my church friends for their encouragement and emotional support. Mrs. McCorkle told me she thought I would be a wonderful Director of Christian Education and that she knew I would do well in college because she could see how focused I was. When Mr. Carruth asked me to provide the music for the summer vacation church school for two weeks, I did not hesitate to say yes, and looked forward to working with him. There were mornings when I thought I was too exhausted to volunteer at church, especially after working two consecutive eight-hour shifts that lasted all night. I knew the music was important to the program and especially to the children, and I did not want to let Mr. Carruth down. I wanted to honor my commitment to the children, too. I would drag myself to church and after engaging the children in singing, my own strength was renewed.

My Sunday School teacher, Mr. Rice, contacted the Director of Admissions at the College of Wooster, (a presbyterian college, south of Cleveland, Ohio). He convinced the Director I was a good student, and he would vouch for my determination to work hard. He said the school could count on me to fulfill all my obligations because I was resolute in my goal for a degree. I applied and was accepted. With scholarship assistance from three sources: my church, the presbyterian denomination, the College of Wooster, and the promise of part-time work there, my dream of going to college was beginning to feel real. After working at Western Union for fifteen months, September finally came. I withdrew my savings, counted my money, and made my train reservation.

I asked my father to drive me to the train. As we approached the New York Central station, he told me that my mother was pregnant, and the baby was due in December. This would be their eighth child. I was furious! I thought at first this was another attempt to keep me at home. My mother was back in the hospital so I knew she must have gotten pregnant during the time she was at home a few months earlier. I was angry with him. I felt he should have taken responsibility to not have any more children, especially when it was clear Mom was unstable after the lobotomy.

He said she would have the baby in the state hospital, and he did not know what would happen to it. He said he definitely would not allow it to be adopted, and he had been told the hospital would not allow Mom to keep the baby at the hospital. I assumed that also meant Mom would not be allowed to name the baby. I knew she had always wanted "American" names for her babies. Dad would probably give the baby an "Italian" name, after one of his brothers or sisters. I felt sad for the baby and for Mom, and disgusted with Dad. I blamed him for this new baby.

He told me, "The doctor said maybe if she had a baby she'd get back to be mother to her children."

This sounded strange to me, but I did not challenge him. I did not want to argue with him just as I was leaving home.

He took my suitcases from the truck, and we entered the busy train station. We hugged each other as we said good-bye and as I climbed the steps of the train he said, "*Stata tenda!*"—the familiar expression he always used when we left the house. He added, "I will send you some money to pay for your train ticket to come home for Christmas."

Surprised by his offer, I said, "Thanks, I'd appreciate the help with the ticket." This would be the only assistance I would receive from him during my four years of college.

However, I was still angry about the news of a new baby, and at the same time so glad to be leaving home. When I found a seat, I breathed a sigh of relief as the train pulled away from Syracuse. I was really on my way. I pondered what Dad had said about the new baby, and wondered what would become of it and what kind of future would it have. How would it help my mother to have an infant but not be able to care for it? Would the doctor let her return home with the baby if no one was there to take care of Mom? There were so many questions that had no answers, but I was determined to begin to concentrate on what my life would be like in college. Finally, I could focus on my own life, and the dream I had made come true: college.

The first few weeks were busy meeting my new roommate and other classmates, becoming familiar with the tree-lined campus, signing up for classes, trying out for the choirs, meeting my advisor, and attending several receptions for new students. I even met the college President, Howard Lowry. Sometimes I felt I should pinch myself: it was really happening, I was attending college!

Being assigned to a small dorm seemed to bring the thirty of us girls closer together. My experience living at Elmcrest with twenty-seven girls gave me a feeling of comfort in the dorm. The other girls often turned to me with questions. They seemed to recognize I was more mature than most others there, and soon I was elected dorm president. I was too busy to think about home, except at night when I said my prayers.

During my four years of college, I was a waitress in one of the dining rooms, becoming head waitress the last two years. In addition, I worked part-time as secretary to the retired president of the college, Dr. Wishart. Most of my time was spent in the music department with courses in music theory and appreciation, history, and conducting. I joined two choirs, both of which rehearsed in the evening. I thought of Mrs. Sheard, and felt confident as a result of her lessons to be singing soprano as we rehearsed the Brahms *Requiem* during my first year. In the spring, the Girls Chorus went on tour throughout the midwest. It was exciting for me to see more of Ohio and Indiana, and finally the second largest city in the country, Chicago. I sent postcards to my father who had never been farther west than Buffalo. We were always warmly welcomed in the presbyterian churches where we sang. Our concerts were well attended and the churches usually provided refreshments where we met some of the members.

Though I spent much of my time in music, I had a double major in psychology and Spanish (thinking that it would be an easier language for me because of my knowledge of Italian). My minor was in music. Through courses in psychology, I learned about the complex factors that contributed to mental illness, and came to understand the sociological, genetic, and behavioral factors in my mother's illness. I wondered if one factor had been the way my father had treated her as a child, and whether having so many children so close together also might have contributed to her illness. It was the first time I had heard about post-partum depression, and I wondered if it might have been an aspect of my mother's problem. Although I still did not share our family story with my classmates, I did have a very sensitive psychology professor whom I confided in. He guided me through the most difficult challenge of my college career —my senior paper. It was called "Independent Study" and every senior could not graduate without successfully completing IS. Recognizing my interest and determination to go on to seminary, he suggested a research project that would allow me to explore the reasons that some of my fellow students chose to enter the ministry. I learned how to do research—formulating the idea, setting up the interview structure, and using the Q-sort method to analyze the data. I selected the subjects to be interviewed, and explored the hidden reasons for selecting the vocation of ministry.

With my advisor's guidance my IS project was successful and gave me the foundation for graduate work. I was proud of what I had accomplished and confident of my new research skills.

During my four years of college, two of my classmates invited me to their homes for weekends and for some of the holidays when I was unable to return home. One family I became very close to were the Hunkes. Their daughter, Joanne, was a waitress in my dining room, and she sang in the same choirs I did. Another classmate, Marjorie, had grown up in Wooster. Her family, former missionaries, invited students to their farm for special meals. One time we helped them plant Christmas trees at the farm after which we were rewarded with a delicious country dinner. I really appreciated being in these comfortable homes, having home-cooked meals, and getting to know parents who took such interest in the activities of us college students. Marjorie's mother must have recognized my need to have a closer connection and invited me to drop in for a cup of tea some afternoons. I cherished the warmth of our teatime together and loved hearing about her missionary experiences in Iran.

I was still in my first year in college when Rosalie and my Dad began calling me to complain about David who was now fifteen. They were worried that David's rebelliousness would land him in a juvenile detention facility. Daddy said David was drinking beer, smoking, and staying out until three in the morning.

He told me, "I don' know what to do with him, he won't obey me, you gotta do somethin." Rosalie said she thought David might be taking money from the offering plate at church. He did not have any money or a job, and Daddy did not believe in "allowances."

I couldn't believe they were expecting me to fix things when I was in Ohio several hundred miles away from home. I reminded Rosalie and Dad that I was in the middle of my first year, and I could not leave college.

I told Rosalie, "I'd be losing all the money I paid for tuition if I left now." She said, "I understand, but I don't know what to do, and Daddy doesn't either." I listened to Rosalie and suggested she talk to one of the ministers at our church for some guidance.

When the Hunkes asked how things were at home, I told them about the problems my Dad and David were having. They wondered aloud if it would help if they took David into their home. They had raised one son who was now in the Air Force and Joanne was in college with me. They had an extra room and felt they could handle a teenaged boy. I was very surprised that they made such an offer to help my family, especially David, whom they had never met. I had never expected such a response when I discussed the problems at home.

Early that summer they arranged to drive from Cleveland to Syracuse to meet my Dad and David. If they were willing, the Hunkes would bring David back to Lakewood to live with them. My father made no mention of money to help support David. Mr. and Mrs. Hunke offered to pay for all his expenses, and would enroll him in the local high school. I could not believe how generous they were. I had never met anyone like the Hunkes, so willing and eager to provide a possible solution for us. Dad was relieved that he did not have to worry about David. I was pleased that I would see David often, and I prayed that this arrangement would work out for everyone. I began to think of the Hunkes as angels sent by God.

David thrived in the new Ohio environment. He had grown to be six feet tall and was handsome with dark brown curly hair and brown eyes. David was a good athlete and spent some time earning spending money as a caddy on a golf course in Lakewood. My brother had such a delightful sense of humor that he made friends easily.

All was well for about two years until David again rebelled, and no longer observed the Hunke's rules and their curfew. Eventually, the Hunkes went to their pastor with their concerns and complaints. Despite his rebelliousness, David had a captivating personality and had endeared himself to everyone he met. The Lakewood pastor found another home for David, which would allow him to remain at Lakewood High. He was fortunate to have the support of the minister of the Lakewood Presbyterian Church and some other parishioners who gave him the guidance he needed.

I did not know of the problems the Hunkes had been having with David until he was in a new home. I was disgusted and horrified that the Hunke's generosity had been treated with such disregard by David, and I was hurt that he had taken advantage of my friends.

The following summer, a member of the Lakewood church

hired David to work on the ore boats that travel the Great Lakes carrying tons of coal and steel between the major ports of Chicago, Cleveland, Detroit, and Buffalo. He became trustworthy and a hard worker, loading and unloading the ore boats every summer. Perhaps the hard work helped him decide to go to college and would give him more options for his future. For five years he spent the summer months on the ore boats earning enough money for college. One year he stayed on the ship until December when the ice closed the channels and all shipping was halted. By then, he was saving money for graduate school. He had turned his life around and was becoming a mature adult. I felt encouraged by the way he was living his life, despite the fact he still engaged in mischievous activities in college.

During my senior year, David joined me at Wooster as a freshman. He too found work in one of the dining rooms and was managing his money fairly well. We delighted in seeing each other on our way to classes, in the library and singing together in one of the choirs. We would talk about our professors, and he began exploring whether he would major in history, a love of his, or the sciences. He also explored a possible career in medicine. We celebrated our birthdays together again as we had done growing up since they are one day apart. It was a good year for both of us. Finally, I could stop worrying about him.

One day in the autumn of 1954, when I was in my last year of college, Rosalie called to tell me that our father had been arrested and convicted of molesting a neighborhood child. He was scheduled to serve as much as eighteen months in the minimum security prison in Auburn, New York. I was devastated and sick to my stomach as I tried to make sense out of what she'd told me. I was too ashamed to share our family's latest disaster with anyone. Although Rosalie did not give me the details, I was furious with my father. She said she had been told that he would probably be released in a few months, but not before Christmas. The warden of the prison was the captain my father had saved during the First World War in France. He remembered my father, and assured my sister that he would look after him. With good behavior he would probably qualify for an early release. Rosalie was newly married and Charlotte was thirteen years old when they visited him at Auburn. Again, my father had become a big disappointment and a source of shame. I thought that at least David and I did not have to tell anyone at college what our father had done, but our sisters and brothers were not so fortunate. They were humiliated that everyone at Elmcrest, at school, and at church knew because of the newspaper account.

Meanwhile, David, a freshman at Wooster, continued to be a ringleader of the practical joke crowd, so I was not surprised when I learned he and a few of his friends had stolen a pig, greased it, and let it loose in one of the girls' dorms one night. They ran away, leaving chaos and confusion behind as the girls and the housemother attempted to capture the pig and remove it from the dorm. I worried that David would get into trouble but his friends covered for him.

As the Christmas holidays approached, all our college friends were going home and we did not want to tell anyone we did not have a home to go to. Our father was in prison and our home had been rented. Rosalie and her husband had just moved to Texas, Ron was in the Air Force, and the other kids were still living at Elmcrest.

When I wrote to tell Aunt Fay and Grandma that we had no place to stay for Christmas vacation, they invited us to stay with them for those two weeks. What a relief. We slept on the floor in their tiny three-room apartment, and tried to be sensitive to their limited food budget. During those two weeks I returned to Western Union to replace a clerk who was on vacation and helped David and me scrape enough money together to give Aunt Fay and Grandma small Christmas gifts of food. We both were grateful for a place to stay, and chuckled that we were probably the only college students sleeping on the floor during the Christmas break.

David spent much of the vacation playing basketball at one of the nearby schools, visiting our sisters and brothers at Elmcrest, and wandering around Syracuse with some of his old friends whom he had not seen in several years. I gave him a little of the money I had earned at Western Union, but we both were frugal, saving just enough to get us back to Wooster, Ohio in January.

Later in January, I received word that I had been accepted at Hartford Seminary in Connecticut. My dream of becoming a

Director of Christian Education would become a reality after I completed the two years of seminary.

As college graduation approached, other students were looking forward to their parents attending the ceremony, but I had no parents who could attend. Immediately after his last class, David had returned to the ore boats, determined to earn as much money as possible. Although he had just completed his freshman year, he was already planning for graduate school.

I decided to invite my sisters and brother who were still at Elmcrest to come to my graduation. I was hoping to encourage them to plan for college and this would be a good time for them to see the campus. I sent bus fare to Doris and Francis, who were the only ones able to come. I enjoyed showing them the campus and introducing them to my friends. They stayed in my dorm and seemed to have fun pretending to be "in college." They asked a lot of questions about Wooster: where I worked, how I had earned the money for school, and where David had lived. They wanted to know what they would need to do to go to college. They had seen how hard I had worked and were proud that I had accomplished my goal of a higher education. I was pleased that they were asking the right questions and were interested in planning for education beyond high school, which was my dream for them.

Because I did not have transportation for the three of us to return to Syracuse, the parents of my former roommate, invited us to drive back to their home in western Pennsylvania where we spent the night. I thanked Isely and her parents again for making it possible for my sister and brother to come to my graduation by driving us part way back. The next day, Doris, Francis and I continued our long trek, changing buses several times until we reached Syracuse.

By the time I graduated, I had paid all my financial obligations. That was a real accomplishment.

I returned to work at Western Union that summer and to Grandma's living room floor. Working double shifts many days and nights I saved enough money for my two years at Hartford Seminary. Rosalie and her husband Bob had moved back to New York State and agreed to drive me and my belongings to Hartford.

On our way, we were astonished to see refrigerators and cars hanging from trees, the remains of a violent hurricane that had struck New England just weeks before. Each time we went around another curve in the road we witnessed more devastation.

Bob began to ask me, "Are you sure you want to go to Hartford? It looks pretty bad. We could turn around and return to Syracuse."

I appreciated his concern, but I was determined to push on to Hartford Seminary.

We finally arrived and were relieved to find that the Seminary was intact and my room was ready for me to move in. I thanked Rosalie and Bob, hugged them, said good-bye, and proceeded to settle into my new "home."

As I had at Wooster, I worked in the seminary dining room and had other part-time jobs, along with a scholarship from the presbyterian denomination. I lived in the women's dorm in a comfortable suite I shared with my roommate, Marcia. All of us students had assignments in neighboring churches on the weekends. My first year internship was at a large congregational Church in downtown Hartford, and my second year at another congregational Church in one of the suburbs. I would travel by bus on Saturday morning to the small town of Marlborough, where the minister would meet me and drive me to the home of one of his parishioners where I would spend the night.

I spent Saturday afternoons meeting with church school teachers or training a small group in how to use the church's curriculum for Sunday School. Guided by the pastor, I would advise the adult leaders of the youth groups, who were working on a project to raise money to send heifers to an African country through a UNICEF program of the United Nations. I was gaining experience in what a Director of Christian Education does.

Seminary was a different experience from college. Classes were small, usually less than twenty students. For the first time, I had begun to date. I had not had any boyfriends in high school or college, so this was a new experience for me. My roommate, Marcia, and I were very popular with the men who took us to basketball games, the movies, to Elizabeth Park, or just to study together. I was enjoying attention from the young men, who all seemed surprised that women were enrolled in the seminary. Unlike today, during the fifties there were no women preparing for the ministry. Most women were studying to become Directors of Christian Education as I was, or preparing for the mission field.

I reveled in male attention, sometimes having three dates in an evening. I made friends with the many foreign students who came to Hartford Seminary and went out with students from Africa, the Philippines, Korea, and Egypt, and dated eight American students during my two years in Hartford. I learned a lot about their countries and what they hoped to do when they returned home. One South African man enjoyed teasing me that when the revolution came to South Africa, he would allow me to be his servant. I did not understand what he was saying, although I knew a little about the apartheid situation in his home country. Then he explained that during apartheid the blacks were servants in white homes but after the revolution that would eliminate apartheid, whites would be servants in black homes. In later years, I often wondered what life was like for him when he returned to South Africa.

The foreign students who had left their families at home were lonely for companionship. Four of us young women, Marcia, Gerry W., Lisa from the Phillipines and I became fast friends, spending a lot of time together not only in class, but collaborating on assignments. We would talk about the men we were dating, compare our college experiences, and share what led us to seminary. We commiserated about assignments, and tried to help each other when we struggled with issues in our field work.

When we felt the need for socializing, we'd advertise that there would be a birthday party for St. Paul or some other Biblical character. All the students would attend and we'd have music, refreshments, and dancing. Some of the men were in a YMCA basketball league and we young women would ride along and cheer them on. A number of older women were working on their Christian Education degrees, as well, but the four of us—Marcia, Lisa and the two Gerrys—were about the same age and had more in common.

Phillip, who was from the Coptic Church in Egypt, teased

me when I proudly told him I had stayed in the home of a parishioner whose house was built in 1804, and the number appeared above the front door. He scoffed, "Egypt has houses that are thousands of years old!"

I laughed. Of course, he was right, America was still a young country compared to Egypt. When some classmate with a car suggested going for coffee, we'd head for Greenwich Village in New York City, a three hour drive, have coffee and return to Hartford in the wee hours of the morning in time to work the breakfast shift in the seminary dining room.

These experiences with men made me realize I was attractive —something I had never thought I could be, but with a childhood of absent parents, poverty, and too many children, I was very cautious with them, not wanting to become too involved. I had my own plans. In order to go to college and seminary, I had made a commitment to my denomination that upon graduation I would work in a presbyterian church for six years, the same amount of time their scholarship had helped me. This allowed me freedom from paying back the money I had received. This debt was always in the back of my mind when I thought of my future, and marriage was not part of my plan.

During seminary, I didn't have the constant worries about my sisters and brothers or my finances. I was enjoying all my classes and the friends I was making.

Near the end of my first year, I had begun to rebel against the method of teaching of one of my professors.

Professor Edna was the most powerful person in the Christian Education program. She wielded more authority over the education students than the other professors in the department. She demanded we create a file of titles of books that she felt we would want to consult when we became professionals in the church. This seemed like a waste of time to me and I refused to do the assignment. Because of this, I failed the course and was forced to repeat it.

All girls have to find ways to separate from their mothers to become their own persons. Professor Edna was the maternal figure I needed to separate from, finding my path to independence by refusing to complete her assignment. Of course, at the time I was not aware of the meaning of my relationship with her.

In December of my second year of seminary, I received a job offer from Herb Schroeder, a minister whom I had known in Syracuse. He had become the minister of the First Presbyterian Church of Watertown, New York, about fifty miles north of Syracuse. He had watched me grow up at Elmcrest and said he had been impressed by my leadership and maturity as a teenager. He hired me to be the Director of Christian Education of his twelve-hundred member church. I was pleased to be the first in my class to have found a position and to be near Syracuse, which would allow me to be more in touch with my brothers and sisters.

I finished seminary in May of 1957 and arranged for my diploma to be mailed to me. I was eager to begin working, although I was apprehensive about leaving my friends and the familiarity of the seminary. Yet, I knew it was time to move on.

CHAPTER TWELVE

PRISON VISIT

*I*t was early summer of 1956, the summer between my two years in seminary, when I found myself in a car on the way to Attica prison with friends of Aunt Fay. They had agreed to drive me because I had no other way to get there. How I dreaded this visit. What made it worse was the fact that this was the second time my father had been sent to prison for molesting a young girl. The first time he had been sent to a minimum security prison, Auburn. Now he was in Attica, a maximum security prison in western New York State. I had not seen my father in more than four years, since before he had been arrested, and I had never been to a prison.

My mind still could not grasp the gravity of what he had done. I didn't really want to see my father, but I felt obligated to visit him. After all, he was my father and I was the oldest in the family. Throughout my childhood he had always expected me to take more responsibility than the rest of my sisters and brothers, and I now had the same expectations of myself.

I tried to control my anxiety by looking out the car window and conversing with Aunt Fay's friends. We all took Jesus' words seriously: "When I was in prison, you visited me." Being faithful to those words led us to Attica, where my father had been incarcerated for two years.

In the real world it was a beautiful sunny day, but for me it felt like a dark night. I did not know what to expect. No one had ever described a prison visit to me. I didn't recall seeing anything on television or in the movies that would have prepared me for it. I was humiliated, torn between the haunting words of Jesus admonishing us to visit those in prison, and my painful feelings of obligation to my father.

As they drove the one hundred and fifty miles west from Syracuse toward Buffalo to Attica, I could hardly put my mind around what I was doing. I had visited my mother in a locked institution. Now I was about to visit my father in another locked institution. This was more painful and embarrassing than when I had visited my mother. How could I ever tell anyone? I couldn't bear to put words to what my father had done, even to myself. As we drew closer to Attica, my stomach tightened and my forehead began to sweat.

All of us children and Aunt Fay were reluctant to talk about the circumstances surrounding my father's imprisonment. None of us felt we could confide even to close friends that both of our parents were institutionalized.

Dad's first prison sentence had been eighteen months to two years, for molesting a child in our neighborhood. I had been a sophomore in college when Rosalie had written that one of the neighbors had reported Daddy to the police for molesting their thirteen-year-old daughter. None of us could believe it. I called Rosalie immediately, and reluctantly offered to drop out of school and return home. The whole family relied upon me to manage difficult situations and I took it for granted that I should be home to take on the latest challenge. However, Aunt Fay said, "There's really nothing you can do here. Stay where you are. The younger children are safe at Elmcrest, and Rosalie will see to renting the house."

I breathed a sigh of relief. Since no one in Wooster knew about our family's latest secret, I went on studying, singing in the college choirs, and going to church as usual. Now, four years later, it was worse--a second offense. This time his sentence was two to six years, and he could not depend on a friendly warden in Attica as he had in Auburn.

How could our father have done such a terrible thing? We told ourselves that, because he had such broken English, people didn't understand him and may have misinterpreted his words and actions. But deep in our hearts, we were forced to believe that the police must have discovered some truth in the neighbor's accusation. Daddy, a child molester!?

As we approached Attica, I saw the guards in the towers with their guns trained on both the visitors' entrance and the inmates. Why were they aiming at the visitors? Did they think we would try to somehow free the inmate we were visiting? Were they trying to intimidate us with their weapons turned on us? I began to tremble. I wiped the perspiration from my forehead, pretending that the heat of the day had caused it. My friends were not going into the prison. I was going in alone.

At the door, I was finger-printed, along with other visitors. The guard searched me, my purse, pockets, and clothing. Another guard asked me to complete a visitor form, and questioned me about my address and my relationship with the inmate I wanted to visit. I hated to put into words on that paper, under the glaring light, that I was visiting my own father. The dozen other visitors did not talk to each other and kept their eyes down, as I did. When the guards were satisfied that we were not bringing any contraband to our loved ones, they herded us into a small room where we were to wait for the inmates to be brought into the visiting area. I sat in nervous silence for more than an hour. Finally, the doors clanged open and a few men came into the visiting room. One of them was Daddy, holding up his pants because they had taken away his belt. My heart sank and I felt like crying.

He shuffled in wearing prison khakis, his feet in shackles. He did not smile, but his eyes conveyed pleasure to see me. He said, wiping his eyes with a red handkerchief, "Hello, honey."

I was in turmoil. Seeing my father humbled made me feel sick. I wanted to put my arms around him. At the same time I wanted to yell, "Why did you do it?"

The prisoners and visitors sat on either side of a thick glass wall about seven feet high. We picked up the telephone to talk to each other, aware that the guard sitting at a higher level at one end of the room was watching every move and listening to our conversation. The noise of everyone talking seemed to drown out private conversations. We had a half hour to talk, but I didn't know what to say. We stared at each other for several long moments.

The guard made periodic announcements. "No reaching above the barrier! No touching the barrier! Quiet down!"

Breaking the silence, Daddy asked about each of the kids. He kept wiping his tears as I told him everyone was fine.

He said, "You know, when I know you Momma would no' be the same again,—after the operation on her head —I shoulda divorce her. Lotsa people say I should. Lotsa dona (Italian women) wana marry me, I know you kids wouldno' like, so I di'n't. Mebbe I wouldno' be here, bu' wha'ya gonna do?"

This was the first I had heard that he had contemplated divorcing our mother. But was he saying that we bore some of the responsibility for his molesting a neighborhood child? It didn't make sense to me. I found it hard to imagine he'd even contemplated divorce. Was he excusing himself by saying that he needed a mate to fulfill his sexual appetite and when he didn't have one, he used a child? At that moment, I loathed him.

I said, "I thought you said you asked the neighbor girl to iron some clothes to take the burden off Doris and Charlotte."

He nodded his head, "Yeh, I was try to help Doris and Charlotte so they not have to iron when they come home on Sundays. I don' know what got into me. Wha' ya gonna do?" His attitude was like shrugging his shoulders. He shook his head and sighed.

I thought to myself, you were an adult, you could have said, I won't touch her. But instead you took advantage of the girl, who was young and innocent. No one else was at home and she was willing to iron clothes in return for some pocket money. She probably trusted him, but he must have coerced her, perhaps offering her more money or a candy bar. My face must have conveyed my thoughts.

"I din't hurt her," he said.

"Then why are you here?"

He wiped away his tears and just looked at me, shaking his head and staring at the floor.

How was I to cope with the knowledge that his intent was to relieve his daughters, but he coerced another girl to fulfill his sexual needs? It still didn't make sense.

I looked around at the other visitors and inmates, some with tears streaming down their faces, others in animated conversation.

After a few minutes of not talking, I asked him, "What do you do all day?"

"I study my Bible and talk to other men to 'bring em to the

Lord.' Two or three don't make fun of my English and they respect me because I know the Bible."

It seemed a strange paradox. He was very religious, and we children had always thought he lived on such a high moral plane. At home, when he finished reading the newspaper each evening, he always turned to the Bible, encouraging us to live according to the teachings of Jesus. How could he have violated a child in such an unspeakable way after all the advice and admonishments he had given us?

I was sickened, I hated having a father who had molested a child, but he was my father, and I felt I should be able to forgive him. After all, I had been able to make allowances in the past when he'd beaten Mom and my brothers. I was able to understand him even when he violently objected to my going to college. Would I ever be able to forgive him for this? I felt lost in a thicket of feelings.

I wanted to ask, "Why did you do it? How could you?" But I couldn't. Perhaps I was afraid of what more he might say that I didn't want to know. This was about sex, and we didn't talk about sex in our family. Then I remembered an incident late one night when I was a young child. I heard my mother yell at my Dad, "Don't touch me, you're like an animal!" I had no idea what she meant then, but now I did. She must have been objecting to his sexual demands. Maybe he had forced the little girl as he had forced Mom to have sex, even when she did not want it. Fortunately, he had not taken advantage of my sisters or me.

He kept talking about the prison routine, telling me they saw lots of movies. There was no television in prisons at that time.

He laughed, "I really lika Marilyn Monroe films."

I was astonished that movies were shown in prison, and amazed that he actually enjoyed watching the sex goddess. My father and his church friends thought that movies would lead us into sin. He had never allowed us to go.

Mom had other ideas. She would sneak us out of the house on a Saturday afternoon with a few coins she somehow had saved, and whisper, "Don't let your dad know you went to the movies." He told us movies would put bad thoughts into our heads. Now he was enjoying those sinful movies in prison. Another paradox!

My father told me how much he enjoyed listening to the Christian radio programs that were broadcast in the prison.

"I lika sing with Billy Graham 'How Great Thou Art, you know." He smiled. He loved to sing. "The men don' let me sing in my cell, I can only sing in the chapel."

I learned there were racial tensions in the prison, and despite his Christian background, his own prejudices surfaced when he said he had never been with so many Negro men and that he found most of them less educated than he was.

"I try to teach 'em the Bible, but they no read good as me an' laugh the way I talk."

The visit ended on as positive a note as it could get. With pride, he showed me his new gold fillings and assured me that his teeth were in splendid condition. Dental students were brought into the prison to practice on the inmates' teeth.

When our half hour was up, the guard announced over the speaker, "Prisoners, step away from the barrier and line up in front of the door."

We were not allowed to hug or touch our loved ones before they were led away. Then the guard ordered, "Visitors, line up in front of the visitors exit." Our handbags and other items that had been taken from us were returned.

As my friends drove me back to Syracuse, I pondered the visit. When my father told me he had been thinking about divorcing my mother, he implied he was entitled to have a sexual partner. Since my mother was no longer available, he must have felt justified in divorcing her and remarrying. I had such a mixture of feelings: he was my father, but I was unsure that I still loved him. I hated what he had done. I was angry with him, humiliated. He had shamed our whole family.

It was true that all of us would have been very upset had he divorced Mom, and I wouldn't have approved of such a radical move. We were still hoping that Mom would be able to come home and we would be a family again. Perhaps it was a fantasy, but we had nothing else to hang onto.

When my brothers and sisters asked about my visit, I told them he was in good health, he had a couple of new gold fillings that he was proud of; that he studied the Bible every day; and he enjoyed Marilyn Monroe movies. I did not tell them that Daddy had considered divorce in order to marry someone else. No one asked if he had explained why he'd exploited the neighbor girl.

That was my only visit to my father during the four years he was in Attica. Despite my ambivalence and shame, we corresponded regularly and he sent many Bible verses, which I faithfully looked up. I was convinced he was sending me special messages through these voices from the Bible. When he wrote to my sisters and brothers, he always insisted they look up the verses, too. We tried to understand this as a way of getting us to use our Bibles, or perhaps, he thought this was a more powerful method of conveying his thoughts and desires——to have the Biblical words speak for him.

In one letter he urged me to read Acts 12:5 "So Peter was kept in prison but earnest prayer for him was made to God by the church." And Matthew 19:26 "But Jesus looked at them and said to them, 'With men this is impossible, but with God all things are possible.'"

It seemed to me he was urging me and our church to pray for his early parole, because "with God all things are possible." The intent of the verse seemed to imply none of us should be discouraged. I presumed that because he was convicted twice, he would not be given early parole.

His closing words in one letter were from Second Corinthians 5:10:"For we all must appear before the judgment seat of Christ, so that each one may receive good or evil, according to what he has done in the body." (The reference to the body refers to The Church, not a person's physical body. My brothers and sisters decided that Daddy was referring to his own body.) Perhaps he was telling us that we should not condemn him because he would be judged in the next life.

I was not the only one who visited our Dad. Our cousins, Charlie and Sally, took Ronnie to Attica for two visits, but none of his other children visited him.

During the following months, I began to wonder if Daddy had a secret past that Aunt Fay and Grandma knew about, which was why they disliked him. They never said anything bad about him to me, but I could always feel their cold silence when I said anything positive about him. Once I'd bragged that Daddy had agreed to pay for my round trip train fare to return home from college for Christmas vacation. They'd said nothing in response. Aunt Fay avoided him when they saw each other at my recitals and at my high school graduation.

All along Aunt Fay, Grandma, and Grandpa must have known something about Daddy's past but never had said anything to me or my sisters and brothers. I began to realize that their silence was a gift. What would I have felt about him had they told me something horrible about him when I was a child? I might not have been able to handle my disgust and hatred of him. No one told me anything about our father's past, but I suspected that he must have had a 'past.'

Even today, my father remains a mystery to me. I wonder what happened to him as a child in Sicily. He had told us his father beat him and his four brothers. I know it was a different culture and time, but I have to wonder if there was more that he did not tell us.

Many years after he was released from prison, I visited him in Sicily at his sister's home. I noticed that the older men frequently went for a walk into the woods or the fields with a young girl. I saw my Dad walking with a young cousin, and wondered about their relationship. Could it be happening again? The thought was too painful to contemplate.

Now, over forty-five years later, when I hear of the arrest of molesters, I shudder. From my brothers' experience at Elmcrest and my work as a family therapist, I know the trauma a molester can cause. I also know how the shame and humiliation affects the molester's family.

As a therapist, I have learned that many molesters have been molested themselves as children and are repeating the trauma as adults. I have had to confront the reality that my father himself may have been molested as a child. That does not excuse his behavior, but helps me to appreciate the mystery that surrounds him.

As I struggled with the problem of forgiveness, I became aware that I had been more concerned with how our family was affected by my father's crime than how the neighbor girl felt. I was sorry for the little girl. I knew her family must be outraged and probably not ever able to make peace with him or our family. But could I forgive my father? Would I ever be able to respect him? I remembered the words from the Ten Commandments to "honor your father and your mother." What would that mean for me? Is it possible to honor a father that I could not respect? Would I be able to honor and respect him if I couldn't forgive him? Questions that haunted me that I could not answer.

None of us in our family have ever discussed this problem of forgiveness. However, I was determined not to wallow in resentment, despite my suffering from my father's behavior. Did I have the right to resent him for what he had done to someone who was helpless? How could I get beyond this?

I began to try to appreciate the difficulties of his life --the physical violence he had endured, and perhaps sexual abuse as well, the lack of adequate food during his growing up years in Sicily, the violence he then flung on his brother by cutting off his ear, and the harsh physical discipline he believed was the only way to keep my mother and my brothers in line. I struggled to try to find some compassion in me without condoning his destructive behavior. Because of his devout faith, I expected him to apologize for his behavior but he never did.

My faith in a God who forgives was the touchstone for me to empathize with my father. Throughout my teen years at church I was taught that we believers are forgiven by a just God. This powerful realization changed the way I related to those who offended me, including my father. I could leave my concerns about their behavior in the hands of God.

Gradually, I began to see that Dad was a product of his family. He had limited exposure to other ways of relating to people, and especially those he loved. The paradox is that, though I did not condone what he had done, I pitied him, and was finally able to forgive him. Making allowances for his past seemed to free me from the anguish and resentment I had carried for many years.

David and Jerry
College 1955

CHAPTER THIRTEEN

BECOMING A PROFESSIONAL AND CREATING A HOME

*W*hen I arrived in Watertown, New York, for my first job after seminary, I moved into a three-room apartment near the church and began getting acquainted with a town so small I could walk everywhere. I immediately started to develop an educational program for the church. Several professional women who were members invited me to lunch and dinner, and soon they became my support group. Mary and Florence were avid golfers who insisted I play golf with them. I had played a little in college, and looked forward to learning the intricacies of the game. I loved being outdoors and walking the course with these new acquaintances.

Winter arrives early in northern New York State. It wasn't unusual for the first snow to fall at the end of September. When we couldn't be on the golf course, we would have supper together and play bridge at Florence and Mary's home. From time to time, several other single women from the church joined us. For the first time in six years, I did not have to study. I could relax and enjoy the company of other young women. We were all proud professionals and talked freely about our work. It was eye-opening to see how contented these women were, and how satisfied with their lives, not looking to marriage as a way to fulfill themselves. Except for the Kirks, Charlene and Fred, our youth group leaders during my high school days--and the

Hunkes from college years, I had seen few models of marriage that appeared to be happy. My parents' marriage was certainly not one to emulate. These women offered me an alternative. I appreciated this, since I often felt pressure from relatives to marry, a requirement in Italian families.

Although I was fifty miles from Syracuse, I was still in the habit of monitoring the well-being of my younger sisters and brothers. The day that Charlotte and Fran told me they would be leaving Elmcrest, I was shocked. Elmcrest was in the process of becoming a facility for seriously disturbed children, and the administrators were encouraging families to take back their children. My father was living alone now, and the administrators at Elmcrest believed Fran and Charlotte, thirteen and fourteen, could be released to his custody. Elmcrest had been a safe home for all of us, and while I had lived there only six years, it had been Charlotte's and Fran's home for thirteen and eleven years respectively. By the time he left Elmcrest, Fran was fourteen and growing toward his adult height of six feet. He was handsome, with brown, curly hair, an engaging smile and a charming personality. Because he had lived in a foster home as a baby and then at Hiawatha, the boys' cottage, I had not had as much contact with him as I'd had with Charlotte. She was special to me since I had taken care of her when she was an infant, and through the years when we lived together at Blue Bird.

She was fifteen when she moved back home with Fran, but she seemed younger than Fran. She was very attractive, the prettiest girl in our family with her dark eyes, delicate features, and kinky light-brown hair. Charlotte was shy, and went through a period when she seemed to be afraid of everything, even answering the telephone. Fran was protective of her and often made phone calls for her. During this period, Charlotte was reluctant to try anything new. She had become accustomed to leaning on Rosalie, Doris, and me when we were at Elmcrest.

For so many years Daddy had told us how much he missed having all of his children with him, so I took it for granted he would delight in having Charlotte and Fran at home. I assumed everything was fine, but soon learned that was not the case. Dad prepared the same kind of meal —pasta for supper every night from Sunday until Wednesday, when he made fresh pasta that lasted until Saturday. When Charlotte and Fran complained, Dad's solution was to place fourteen dollars on the dining room table every week. He expected them to buy what they wanted and to prepare their own meals.

Apparently, this had gone on for a few months before I went home for a brief visit and Charlotte told me everything. I was appalled. She said that she and Fran had tried to negotiate what to buy, but neither of them had had any experience at Elmcrest of buying food or preparing meals. I tried to intervene with Dad, explaining to him what Charlotte and Fran needed, but he would not bend.

For about a year, they had managed by themselves. They went to school every day as they were supposed to, but they found it impossible to get a decent breakfast or prepare their school lunches with the money he'd allotted them. They began fighting about the money, unable to agree about how to manage their meals. Daddy didn't intervene, choosing not to notice their difficulties while continuing to prepare his own meals and lunches. He had washed his hands of them.

Again, I urged Dad to change the way he was managing, or rather, not managing the meals for the three of them. His response was disheartening. He couldn't tolerate their complaints about having pasta every night. He said it was good enough for him and it should be good enough for them. I tried to explain the need for more balanced meals, but he was not interested in making any adjustments in the way they were living. I had the sense that he found them a nuisance.

Fran decided he would take $7, and told Charlotte she could have the other $7, so they could be on their own and wouldn't have to argue about food. Of course, that was not a satisfactory solution. They began to lose weight, became lethargic, and found it difficult to keep up with school work.

During one of my visits home, I came to understand the full extent of Daddy's neglect of Charlotte and Fran. I decided something had to be done.

I did a mental inventory of our family: Rosalie and her husband had moved back to Texas for his work. David was in graduate school at Ohio State and recently married. Ronnie had just been released from the Air Force and was newly married, with a baby on the way. Doris had moved to Elmira, New York where she worked for Mohawk airlines and was frequently moving around. Our youngest brother, Vincent (Buddy) was still living in a foster home. It seemed that no one else could take care of Charlotte and Fran the way they needed to be taken care of. If I took them on, I would be totally responsible for my teenaged brother and sister. At twenty-five, I had mixed feelings about losing my independence, but I was the only one who could make a home for them.

I found a two-bedroom house for rent not far from the church and enrolled them in the high school in Watertown, with great hopes that our problems were solved. But it was not long before Fran began acting out. He found a way to withdraw $100 from my bank account and ran away. I was frantic. With the help of my minister friend, Herb, and the police, Fran was found within two days in Washington, DC and returned to Watertown. I tried to talk with him, but he was sullen. However, he did return to school and did his chores around the house, but he would not keep up with his school work. He was resentful at having been returned to Watertown and to my custody. The tension was high between us.

There were some good times, too. Charlotte and Fran were popular. They developed friends at school and went to football games together. At Thanksgiving, two of my seminary friends were coming to bring the car I was buying and to spend the holiday with us. Charlotte, Fran, and I were eager for their visit to help break the tension in our household. Fran was always on his best behavior when we had guests.

While Fran and Charlotte went to the football game, I began preparing some of the dishes for Thanksgiving dinner. I started the stuffing and baked pies while I waited for Art and Marcia to arrive. I placed a dozen chestnuts in the oven for the stuffing, but soon heard loud popping. I opened the oven door and chestnuts came jumping out! I didn't know I should have cut an X into them so they could expand in the roasting. What a mess we had cleaning chestnuts off the kitchen walls and ceiling, but it was worth hearing everyone's compliments about how much they enjoyed our Thanksgiving dinner. Charlotte, Fran, and I were glad to have Art and Marcia with us. I was particularly pleased to buy Marcia's station wagon. Over the next few months, I took driving lessons and then enjoyed the freedom of my new car.

We had some close calls when the snowdrifts at the street intersections in Watertown reached twenty feet and no one could see if traffic was coming from the cross streets. However, I quickly learned that every driver placed a colored plastic ball on the car antenna to alert other vehicles approaching an intersection. One had to be cautious driving in a town that prided itself on receiving one hundred inches of snow before Christmas.

When I realized my salary couldn't support all three of us, I began applying for jobs that paid more. Charlotte and Fran understood the constraints of our tight budget and were prepared to move when I found a new position. Within six months I was hired to be the Director of Christian Education in a larger church, John Knox Presbyterian, in Youngstown, Ohio. The salary would be nearly enough to meet our financial needs. The three of us made plans to move to Ohio.

Although I had only recently received my driver's license, I drove the three of us in our new station wagon to Youngstown. It was hundreds of miles in winter weather but I was determined. Charlotte, Fran, and I sang popular songs and hymns most of the way to Youngstown, anticipating a new adventure.

We moved into a spacious two-bedroom, second floor apartment on a tree-lined street within walking distance of the church and the high school. We were all pleased. I was excited about my new job and a place that was considerably warmer than northern New York State.

By now, Charlotte and Fran had changed high schools twice in less than a year. The move took more of a toll on Fran, who'd been having difficulty in school even before the first move. In my attempt to understand and be sensitive to Fran's unhappiness, I remembered that he had been in twelve foster homes during the first two and a half years of his life when Mom first went into the state hospital and he had been too young for Elmcrest. Instability seemed to set him off. It had to be related to his early life. He did not have the essential bonding with his mother during his first two years as the rest of us had been lucky enough to have. I didn't know how to help him with this transition to a new school and city.

Charlotte and I were very close as sisters. We had a lot in common. She was as short as I at only five feet tall, and she was a shy girl, always with a hint of a smile on her face. She would complain to me about her inability to deal with her naturally curly chestnut brown hair until I encouraged her to get it straightened as I did mine. This helped her manage her hair more easily and reduced her complaining. I was relieved to see she had lost her fear of everything, and made friends more easily than when she had first moved from Elmcrest. She realized she needed to contribute to our household and found a part time job in the office of a men's clothing store. We all were pleased when she began to earn money for her own clothes and incidentals.

Though Fran was tall and looked older than fifteen, he was not yet old enough to get a work permit. I encouraged him to study and offered to help him with his homework, but he claimed he had completed it by the time I arrived home from work. Instead of studying, his instability led him to attach himself to a rebellious group of schoolmates who were beginning to experiment with drugs.

I tried to be patient with Fran knowing it must be tough to change schools twice in a year and lose credits. He became more resistant to authority at school and at home. One day he came up the stairs of our home talking to the walls, saying such things as, "Hello walls, how are you today?" Charlotte asked him to whom he was speaking but he ignored her.

When I asked him to be home by ten o'clock on school nights, he'd shout, "You're not my mother!"

Charlotte and I worried about him when we heard him talking to himself or to the walls or to no one in particular. The teachers and principal also became concerned about his behavior. The day he assaulted a teacher, the school had him transported by ambulance to the psychiatric unit of the local hospital, where he was kept for observation and assessment for two weeks.

When he was released, I was surprised when he told us, "There was no problem. I got along well with the nurses and doctors, they all liked me. They didn't think I needed to be there." He may have believed that, but the doctors required him to see a psychiatrist at the mental health clinic located near our home. I was surprised and pleased that he kept his weekly appointments.

It occurred to me that he must have needed an impartial male to talk about the problems he was having with his older sister.

After a few weeks, the psychiatrist phoned me at work one day to warn me that Fran was planning to kill me. I told him I had no idea he was that unhappy or disturbed. He went on to tell me about two incidents Fran had revealed. The first one had occurred in the kitchen; he was preparing dinner and had the butcher knife in his hand. He told the psychiatrist that he almost came at me with the knife. Another time he planned to step on the gas pedal while I was driving. He planned to jump out, and I would be left to crash the car.

The psychiatrist told me, "Take these warnings seriously. Your brother is very angry with you for disrupting his life by taking him away from Syracuse. Be extra careful."

When I hung up the phone, I was stunned, and felt numb. I was still unable to grasp all that the psychiatrist had said. Then I headed for the office of my closest work colleague, Bill, the Associate Minister of the church, to tell him what the psychiatrist had said. Bill was concerned for my safety and urged me to tell Charlotte so she could also be alert and perhaps protect me.

I shared this with Charlotte as soon as she returned from her after-school job. We knew Fran hadn't expressed anger towards her, only toward me. For the next year Charlotte and I checked in with each other daily as we observed Fran. I found some relief talking with Bill. He suggested that Fran might need to get away for a while, and thought I should consider a church-related summer project that he knew about in South America.

As summer approached, Charlotte and I continued to be alert to Fran's behavior and the friends he was hanging out with after school. We three had agreed on a curfew, which Fran began to ignore. I was feeling helpless in disciplining him. He was still only fifteen years old, but he was much taller than I. However, when I suggested he might consider a summer work camp in Ecuador sponsored by the Church of the Brethren, he was delighted with the idea of leaving the country. He said he had always wanted to travel to other places and to get away from Youngstown for a while. Both Charlotte and I looked forward to having a respite from constantly being on guard. My shoulders felt lighter once Fran left, and Charlotte and I talked about how worried we had been for almost a year. We relaxed for the summer.

When Fran returned at the end of August, he seemed different. As we sat around the supper table, he told us the work camp was just what he needed.

"It was great to be outside the United States and to meet so many interesting Ecuadorean people," he said. "There were about twenty-five American kids from different parts of the states. I made a real good friend, his name was Chase, and his parents are very wealthy, they have homes in New York City, in New England, and even in France."

He showed us his arm muscles. "At the work camp we built latrines, and helped the farmers plant vegetables high up on the mountains where they lived. We worked hard but we had fun, too. You would have liked it we did a lot of singing in English and in Spanish."

He presented Charlotte with a beautiful embroidered blouse and gave me a lovely hand-made tablecloth. Seeing how poor the people were seemed to give him a new appreciation for all that he had in America. His new attitude surprised me, and naturally I was relieved that he had changed. He seemed so much happier and more relaxed. For several months, he was cooperative and helpful around the house, took his school work seriously, and seemed glad to be home. He eagerly helped prepare supper every evening and was proud to prepare an Ecuadorean meal for which Charlotte and I enthusiastically praised him.

He took a cooking class at school where he was to prepare a dish that required flour. Since we were almost out of flour, he substituted cornstarch. Of course, his concoction was inedible. I showed him the difference between flour and cornstarch and after buying the flour, he began his project again. I was pleased that he had accepted my suggestions and I felt more relaxed and unafraid when we were in the kitchen together. Charlotte noticed this change in our relationship and told me how comfortable she also had become.

Fran developed some creative recipes. One time, he marinated beef liver in vinegar before frying it with onions. Charlotte and I were impressed with how delicious it was, and complimented him on his creativity. It was such a relief to be getting along better. However, his school performance still concerned me.

I was afraid to push him too much, for fear he would revert back to wanting to kill me. It was a delicate balance of showing interest in his school work but not pressuring him.

I enjoyed my work and the new friends I had made at the church, but at twenty-seven years I found it still a challenge to be raising two teenage children especially one with such mood swings as Francis had.

One winter night, Charlotte gave me a scare. She went with some girl friends on a Friday night outing and had not returned home by midnight. I began pacing, and Fran said he couldn't sleep either, knowing Charlotte was not home. I called the hospital and then the police to inquire if there had been an auto accident. The police assured me that there had not been an accident but the streets were covered with ice. I did not know all of her girlfriends, but Fran gave me a list of the ones he knew. I started calling the parents of some of her friends to see if their daughters had arrived home. It was two-thirty in the morning before I located Charlotte. She confirmed what the police had reported, the streets were too icy to drive so she stayed with one of her girl friends. It had not occurred to her to call home.

One of the parents told me, "How typical of teenagers. They never think to let their parents know what they are doing."

Once I knew she was all right, I couldn't be angry with her. I told Fran I couldn't have found her without him and thanked him for all his help. Finally, we were able to get to bed.

We had been living in Youngstown for two years when our father was released from Attica prison and came to stay with us. He shared Fran's room where there was an extra bed. Fran complained to me about Daddy's snoring, and I reassured him that Dad would only be with us for a short time, perhaps for a couple of weeks. Dad told us he planned to stay only until Doris could send him a free airline pass, a privilege for parents of airline employees. After fifty-two years in the United States, he planned to return to Sicily where he was born. He would spend the winter there and return to upstate New York to spend the summer visiting his children—Rosalie and Ronnie and their families. He was excited to return to his birthplace after so many years. I had mixed feelings. I was glad he was released from prison, and pleased that he could visit us. I wanted him to see how well the three of us were getting along. But we were all relieved he would not be with us long.

We anxiously waited for Doris to arrange for the airline pass. Two weeks turned into four months. I could not understand what was taking so long.

Daddy soon became bored with nothing to do in Youngstown. He studied his Bible and wrote letters to his relatives, but he spent most of the time taking long walks while Fran and Charlotte were at school and I was at work. I turned down invitations to lunch to go home every noon and have lunch with him, and monitor what he was doing. He said he enjoyed the walks and the beautiful trees on our street and had begun to engage with neighbors whom he met on his strolls. I worried that he would become inappropriately involved with children again.

I asked Fran, "Do you think you could spend more time with Dad when you come home from school? You know how much he loves to walk, perhaps, you could take him to the Uptown Shopping area and show him around. I want to be sure that he does not become too friendly with the children in the neighborhood."

Fran said, "I know what you mean. I saw him giving some candy to some of the kids up the street the other day. I'll try to get him to walk with me."

There were days when I felt I had taken in three children. I worried a lot and wondered when Doris would be sending the pass for Dad to be on his way. He wasn't leaving soon enough.

I thought about taking Dad to the church where I worked during the day, but there was nothing for him to do there and I feared that he would get in the way of the ministers and other church staff. I drove the four of us to a Cleveland Indians baseball game, and Dad seemed to enjoy the outing. He had never been west of Buffalo before coming to Ohio. When the Metropolitan Opera performed in Cleveland, I had taken Charlotte and Fran to a performance. I was pleased when they told all their friends and Dad how much they enjoyed the opera, *Der Rosenkavalier*. I was determined to introduce them to classical music and bought records which we played while we ate supper. Fran and Charlotte identified *Liebestraum* and *The Moonlight Sonata*. Dad said, "*Bella cosa!*" (a wonderful thing), impressed with their musical knowledge.

Dad then told me, "I'm glad you went to college. Now you can support Charlotte and Fran and give them an education, too."

The conflict and struggles I had with him over my desire to go to college came to my mind. Finally, he was acknowledging my decision was the right one for me, albeit now that he had handed over his parenting responsibilities to me.

After four months, Doris finally sent the free pass. I drove Charlotte, Fran, and Dad to New York where Doris joined us. As we all watched him board the plane to Rome, we breathed a great sigh of relief. We celebrated his departure at an Indian restaurant in the Village and I treated the four of us to an off-Broadway play. Then Fran, Charlotte and I drove back to Youngstown and Doris returned to Elmira.

Each summer we lived in Youngstown, I drove back to Syracuse to bring Vincent, our youngest brother, for a two week visit. (He was the baby born when my mother had returned to Marcy State Hospital.) We had only seen him occasionally when we were living in Syracuse. His foster family, the Van Marters, were eager for Vince, whom they called Buddy, to have more contact with his brothers and sisters. Vincent was a shy child which made it difficult to find things to talk about. He had a skinny body with thin arms and legs and reminded me of David when he was the same age, but David had been very sociable, talkative, and even entertaining. When Buddy was with us, Fran, Charlotte and I tried hard to find things we could do with him. We had picnics in Mill Creek Park and took him to a ball game in Cleveland. We showed him around our city and surrounding countryside and parts of West Virginia, thinking it would be good for him to know a world beyond Syracuse.

Finding the right food for Vincent was a problem. We were used to eating meals from a variety of cuisines—Mexican, Indian, Middle Eastern, and of course, Italian. Buddy hated rice and it was quite difficult to get him to try new foods. I thought I was doing him a favor by introducing him to a wider variety, but I finally realized that he agonized over meals that he found distasteful. Despite those problems, I was glad we had some time together each summer and helped him feel part of our family.

Buddy had lived with the Van Marter's from the time he was

born, when he'd been taken by a social worker from my mother in the state hospital, so they were the only family he considered his own. He lived with them until he was nineteen years old. I think these summer visits helped him to acknowledge that he had seven brothers and sisters and was part of the Messina family.

Fran was so eager to leave home on his eighteenth birthday that I did not try to persuade him to graduate from high school first. It would have been futile to insist. He was hopelessly behind in all of his classes, except his cooking class. For a short time, he worked in the men's department of a downtown department store in Youngstown. He was convinced it had prepared him for any job anywhere. There was no point arguing with him. Off he went with two of his high school friends, heading to a new life in California. Charlotte and I prayed for him daily, hoping that he would be safe and free from his past troubles. We trusted he'd find a way to make a living for himself.

For more than two years no one in the family heard from Fran. Finally, Charlotte received a post card saying he loved California, his new home, but he gave no return address. We had many questions: What was he doing? Where was he living? How was he supporting himself? When would he return--at least for a visit? Charlotte and I both admitted we missed him. It would be almost six years before he made contact with us again—long after our father had died.

Because Charlotte had attended three high schools in two years, her graduation had been delayed. She was unhappy about losing credits each time she moved to a new school. She'd worked hard as a student, and continued to work part-time in an office after school and on Saturdays. I was feeling proud that Charlotte was doing well, even if Fran was not. I helped her with applications for college, and we both were pleased when she was admitted to Youngstown University and could still live at home.

She did well in college. I enjoyed hearing about her business and economics courses. However, in the middle of her senior year she fell in love and told me she could not concentrate on her studies any longer. I was disappointed, but I knew that young women often dropped out of college for that reason. She began working full time, saving money for wedding expenses, and soon married her high school sweetheart, Dick, who had been active in my youth group at our church. After he returned from the Navy, they rented a house near Youngstown and she continued working. Now her focus was on creating a family. I still hoped that she would finish her senior year and graduate.

Two years later she gave birth to her first baby, a girl named Susan. While Charlotte was in the hospital the nurses prevented me from visiting her. At that time only parents or grandparents of the newborn were allowed to visit. After some wrangling, Charlotte and her husband, Dick, convinced the nurses that because I had been raising Charlotte, I should be permitted to visit. Even though I had never had a baby, I'd had plenty of experience taking care of Fran and Charlotte when they were babies. When Charlotte went home from the hospital I spent a week helping her. It was such a joy taking care of Charlotte and her new daughter. I changed diapers, prepared bottles, and held Susan when she cried. She was so tiny, and reminded me of Charlotte when she was a baby. She had the same eyes and kinky hair. I loved helping Charlotte with Susan and have felt a special bond with Sue ever since. I had also taken care of the newborn children of my brother, Ron, and his wife, Sharon. I was beginning to feel what grandmothers must feel, caring for their new grandbabies. Here was a new generation, and how fortunate I was to take part in welcoming this new baby girl into our family. Charlotte would often tell me, "I couldn't have gotten through that first week without your help."

I assured her, "I enjoyed so much holding Susan and helping you out just as I did with Ronnie's two children. I guess I'm playing the role Aunt Fay played for our mother when we were born." I prayed silently that Baby Susan would not have as difficult a life as her mother did as I thought about Charlotte's twelve years at Elmcrest.

After four years in the Youngstown position, and with both kids finally on their own, I was eager to have my own life. I had developed a reputation for having trained a cadre of excellent teachers and leaders in the church to carry on the educational program I had created. At the age of thirty, I felt I deserved to be free of taking care of everyone else. I was eager to pursue my own dreams. I couldn't wait to travel.

For years I had dreamed of seeing the great art and the cathedrals of France, Germany, England and Italy. From the time my father had returned to his hometown, he had been urging me to visit him in Sicily. His letters piqued my curiosity about where he had grown up and what life was like there. When I was accepted for a study seminar in orthodox theology at the Ecumenical Institute in Bossey, Switzerland, my dreams were about to become realities. Part of the seminar would include attending Russian Orthodox holy week services at the seminary in Paris. I could hardly believe I would be spending three weeks in a chateau in Switzerland and Paris!

A load was being lifted from my shoulders. I put the household goods in storage and sold my car, knowing that when I returned from Europe at the end of six months I would have a new position. I had been hired to be an Educational Consultant on the national staff of the Presbyterian Board of Christian Education. This meant that I would be using my education and experience from my work in Watertown and Youngstown to develop and train local church school teachers to be as creative as public school teachers.

Until the early 60's, many church school teachers had used one method of teaching —lecturing. In seminary I discovered that children and youth had become used to more creative methods of teaching in the public school, and churches were beginning to train their teachers to be more imaginative. I had been training teachers in the church to use films, film strips, play acting, art, and music. I was thrilled to have my work recognized by the national office of the Presbyterian Church. My new job was to begin in September of 1964. First, I would spend five months in Europe, part of the time at the Ecumenical Institute in Bossey, Switzerland and Paris, and then I would visit friends living in Europe. This would also give me the opportunity to accept my father's invitation to visit him in Sicily and to meet my relatives.

CHAPTER FOURTEEN

MEETING THE ITALIAN RELATIVES

*A*fter the Seminar at the Ecumenical Institute, I rented a car in France and drove alone to Torino in northern Italy where I would meet my father, who was visiting one of his nieces there. Then we planned to travel the length of Italy to Sicily, visiting Messina relatives along the way.

I arrived at the outskirts of Torino (Italy's Detroit, where most of its cars are manufactured,) to find it was much larger than I expected. Although it was dusk, I thought it would be easy to follow the map and my father's directions. However, when I arrived at the piazza where my father was supposed to be staying, I could not find my cousin's name on any of the mailboxes at the apartment houses that hugged the square. I inquired at the local bar and the local mom and pop shop. I spoke to people sitting in the piazza, but no one had ever heard of her. I returned to the apartment house of the address my Dad had sent, examining the mailboxes again. Still no luck. By nine that night, I needed to find a place to stay.

From my brief experience in Europe, I had learned that one can always find a hotel near any train station. With my map of Torino, I wound my way to the train station and checked into a small hotel nearby. What would I do if I could not find my father? Should I go to the police? What would they be able to do? I had very little sleep worrying about what I would do the next morning. After a quick breakfast, I checked out of the hotel and headed back to the piazza to begin again the daunting task of trying to find my father. As I climbed out of my car, I heard my name—"Gialdina! Gialdina." I looked up to see my father hanging out of a fifth story window demanding to know where I had been!

He came running down the stairs, hugged me and demanded, "Where you been, what happened to you? You were supposed to be here yesterday! What happened to you?"

I showed him the directions he had sent and he admitted he had given me his niece's maiden name. He said when he had left Sicily in 1913, women often used their maiden name even after they were married, and he had forgotten to give me her married name.

I was furious with him for his mistake which had caused me so much anxiety. I couldn't stay angry. I was relieved to have finally found him. As he had so many times over the years, he elicited such a mixture of feelings in me.

My cousin Rosaria and her three young children warmly embraced me, their American cousin. In spite of my limited Italian, we seemed to communicate well enough as we gathered around the table where she had prepared a delicious minestrone soup for the midday meal. She was a rapid talker and somewhat loud, but very gentle with her three little children. She quizzed her eldest about her day at school and reminded her that there was only one week before summer vacation, admonishing her to be nice to her nun/teacher. Rosaria turned to me and said that near the end of the school year, children tend to become disrespectful of their teachers and liked to tease the nuns.

Rosaria was in her mid-thirties, slightly older than I was, with curly black hair and sparkling eyes. Rosaria had been named after her mother, still a common custom in Italy. She was eager to know what life was like in America. She asked questions in Italian about my sisters and brothers and the inevitable question: why was I not married? I was not surprised she asked. All Italians believe every woman should be married. I tried to explain that I was a working woman, and that many women in America were not married. Since I was using the Italian I had learned when I was growing up, there were times I could not remember the vocabulary and had to rely on my father to translate for us. Gradually, I began to feel more comfortable using the language and did not need my father to explain things to me.

It was next to impossible for Rosaria to understand about my work in presbyterian churches in America. She had no knowledge of protestant churches and of a young woman working to improve the educational program of the church. She could only relate to similarities with the nuns at her child's school. I acknowledged that we were similar, while my Dad tried to explain what protestant churches were.

He asked her, "Have you heard of the Waldensians in Italia?" She nodded.

"Well, they are protestants, they do not look to the Pope as their leader." He turned to me. "Their headquarters are in Rome. I'll take you to the Waldensian church when we visit Rome."

Rosaria could not understand why the Waldensians would not want to follow the dictates of the Pope. Dad tried to engage her in a theological discussion in Italian while I listened. I admired his ability to try to explain something that seemed unbelievable to Rosaria, who frequently shook her head, not understanding what he was saying.

During the visit, I asked Rosaria to show me how to make her delicious minestrone soup. She was surprised that I was interested in cooking. She said she thought all Americans bought ready-made meals like McDonald's. Her kitchen was tiny and had no refrigerator. She insisted she did not need one since she shopped every day for the ingredients needed to prepare the main meal. There was a television, but they did not watch it much while I was visiting.

I read *Pinocchio* in Italian to her children before we tucked them into their beds. Rosaria kept insisting that I should be married and told me how much joy her children brought her. In spite of our very different lives, we genuinely liked each other.

Her husband Louie asked Dad to sponsor him so he could move to America. He said he was a tailor and was sure he could find work. His dream was to go to America and send for his wife and children when he had enough money to pay for their passage. Dad did not seem very enthusiastic and made no promises. Later he told me he thought Louie was not very reliable. He referred to him as a "hot head" and did not pay much attention to his family.

The next few days, Dad took me to view the tombs of the House of Savoy, and then to the Palazzo Royale, the Museum of Torino, where a relic of the shroud of Jesus was displayed in a glass case. At least, that is what it was purported to be. Dad was skeptical.

"How could it be possible that anyone would know it was from Jesus from over two thousand years ago? How can these people believe this? They are too gullible. They believe anything the priest and the Pope says." He was definitely not buying the popular myth, and I agreed with him.

We continued through the galleries, viewing the Renaissance paintings until we arrived at one magnificent portrait of a pope that had been painted by someone with our name, Messina. Dad was thrilled to learn that one of our ancestors had been such a fine painter. I gently told Dad that *"da Messina"* meant that the painter was from the city of Messina, not that his name was Messina. But he preferred to believe the artist was an ancestor.

We traveled on to Voghera, not far from Milan. Dad's niece, also named Rosaria, and her husband, Alfonse Ferante, were considerably older than I was, almost as old as my father. They welcomed me warmly and said how happy they were that we were visiting them. They lived in a tenement where they shared a toilet and bath with several other families. Giuseppe and Alfonse, their two sons in their early twenties, were selling T-shirts at the street market and had plans to expand their business. Their teenaged daughters were in school, worked part-time, and were hoping to go to college. Their seven-year-old daughter, Francine, was blind, had epileptic seizures, and possibly cystic fibrosis. She could not walk and had to be carried by her mother and sisters because they couldn't afford a wheelchair. The other residents of that large tenement often yelled to Rosaria to stop the noise, but the family found it almost impossible to prevent Francine from screaming.

Rosaria sang my father's praises for taking her and Francine by train to see doctors in Milan and then to Rome to get a diagnosis and treatment for her. Sadly, there still had been neither a diagnosis nor treatment, but Rosaria said she was satisfied that she had pursued all possible medical options in Italy.

I wondered how this family of seven managed to live with such poverty and the taunts from their neighbors in the crowded conditions of the tenement. Though I had experienced poverty growing up in a large family, it did not compare to the struggles of this family.

When we packed my little Simca the morning we were to leave, Rosaria and Alfonse gave us two bottles of wine they had made. We knew they were precious but we didn't have much room and I tried to refuse them, but they insisted. My father reminded me that they were gifts, and we dare not reject them. It was their way of thanking us for spending time with them.

We were still packing the car with our luggage, the homemade wine, and a large box of baked goods they gave us, when one of the bottles of wine blew its cork and sprayed the back seat. What a mess and what a smell! We spent the next hour trying to clean out the car. The baked goods were soggy and had to be thrown out. Dad and I apologized for the loss of the wine as we finally climbed into the car to leave. Although we kept the windows open, the stale wine odor stayed with us all the way to Sicily.

In Milano, we visited the famous Cathedral, Il Duomo, and viewed the painting of the Last Supper. When I saw the billboards in front of La Scala, I dreamed of returning someday to attend a concert or the opera. We did not have relatives there, so Dad was eager to drive on to Montecatini Terme where his nephew Calogero, lived with his wife, Margherita, and their two children, Dino and Maria. Montecatini Terme is famous for its mineral springs and spa and is a popular destination for wealthy Europeans and, especially, Middle Eastern royalty. Calogero worked in the "establishments" as he called them, and was fluent in French, German, English, and of course, Italian. He resembled my Uncle Salvatore, back in Syracuse, "*Tzitsi*", a form of "uncle," as we called my father's brother. I could see they were related from their similar short build, balding heads, and round stomachs. Sparkling eyes and gentle voices indicated to me that they definitely were part of the same Messina family.

Dino was short and slim, and appeared to be serious only when he talked about his studies in economics at the University of Bologna. He was eager for me to know that Bologna was where Italian communism was very strong, but he assured us it was quite a different variety from the communism of the Soviet Union. It was more like socialism. Dino was athletic. He ran each morning, and skied in the mountains north of Torino in the winter. He enjoyed swimming in the sea during the summer. Maria, his sister, was always kidding and joking. She was about Dino's height, with dark brown curly hair like mine, and seemed to find humor in most everything. We laughed together a lot. She assured me she was not athletic, but she did like to swim in the sea when they went camping each summer. She was working in a men's store to save money for college and planned to become a teacher.

I noticed that the Italian women I'd met were eager for an education, but only nursing and teaching were options for them. Maria and Dino both made great efforts to speak to me in English when they recognized my Italian was not very good. They enjoyed telling jokes in Italian and often had to explain them to me. We had such fun together, it made me feel I had always known them.

Florence is only about a thirty minute drive from Montecatini and they were eager to show me "their Firenze" and its famous art galleries: the Palazzo Vecchio, Palazzo Uffizi, Palazzo Pitti, Galaria Palatino, Giordino Boboli, the famous formal gardens, as well as Il Duomo with its bronze doors of Paradise. My mouth dropped when they told me it took twenty-seven years to create the first door and twenty-five years for the other one. It was a short walk to the beautiful Baptistry, and then a few streets away to a mausoleum that showcased the sculptures by Michelangelo of *Dawn* and *Dusk*. Unlike some of the sculptures on street corners that were deteriorating from the pollution of the city, Dawn and Dusk were protected, enclosed in a large mausoleum that was still beautiful after almost five hundred years. How could one not be stunned standing in front of the larger-than-life *David*? I had seen copies and photographs, but was brought almost to tears to be confronting the original nude *David*, the muscles of his figure carved into stone. I was amazed that his hands even had fingernails.

Maria and Dino took us into the Galleria Uffizi and selected three or four of their favorite paintings for us to appreciate. I was moved by Titian, (*Tiziano*, they called him) in his portrait called *Young Man with a Glove*. I could see what Maria meant when she said the portrait conveyed so much character. She pointed out the way the eyes followed us no matter where we moved in the gallery. It was almost like a photograph--the shading and the light seemed so real. They were showing me a new way to appreciate Renaissance art. Even my father would stand before a painting and say, "Imagine that? An Italian painted this!"

In the Uffizi Gallery I fell in love with Caravaggio. The way he used illumination in his paintings had a way of drawing the eye toward his subject. *The Sacrifice of Isaac* depicted the Biblical story of how God challenged Abraham to sacrifice his son, Isaac, as a test of his obedience. At the last moment, an angel appeared with a ram to replace Isaac on the sacrificial altar. Caravaggio captured the Old Testament event with his use of light on Isaac's fearful face and Abraham's distracted look toward the angel, who kept him from sacrificing his son. Of course, my father loved being able to tell Maria and Dino the story of Abraham and Isaac. In turn, they pointed out that *chiaroscuro* was what Caravaggio was famous for the distribution of light and shade or shadow to bring drama to his paintings.

When I inquired how they knew so much about art and music, they assured me that every child learned about art and music in school as they were growing up. They had studied and listened to opera, and knew all the famous Italian composers. They showed me where Verdi had lived when he spent summers in Montecatini, and they described the summer musicals in the park.

From my time with Maria, Dino, and their parents, I knew that I would see them again and maintain contact with these new-found cousins. We found a lot to talk about, despite living such different lives.

Throughout my growing-up years, I had hated being Italian and tried to avoid identifying with Italians. I felt all Italians were poor, uneducated, and had little to offer the world except pasta. I was always humiliated when someone would ask me whether my father was part of the mafia. They seemed to assume that anyone from Sicily must be involved in the mafia. I would insist that he was not, but would wonder if they believed me. Almost everyone I met assumed I was Roman Catholic and when they learned I was not, they wanted to know why I wasn't. It was difficult for most people to believe that an Italian-American could be a protestant.

Now these relatives were introducing me to my Italian culture and heritage and I was loving it. Both Dino and Maria added to my limited understanding about the extent that Italians had contributed to art, sculpture, architecture, and music. From my voice and piano lessons, I knew some of the Italian composers like Rossini and Verdi. My father would talk about Caruso, claiming he was the greatest Italian tenor. However, Maria and Dino were introducing me to Gallicurci, Mascagni, and Leoncavallo, who had composed the opera about the sad clown, *Pagliacci*. I told Dino I thought he should be Italy's Minister of Culture, he was so well educated in the arts. He laughed and insisted that everyone in Italy grew up developing pride in the Italian composers and artists.

While we were visiting in Montecatini, Calogero and his brother, Pietro, began sharing stories about their experiences in World War II. After an evening meal, we sat around the table as they told us about being involved in the resistance movement while they were in the army. They were proud "partisans," as they were called, and famous for sabotaging the German occupation.

They told how the Italian soldiers hated their German captain, who had taken over from their beloved Italian leader. They knew he could be dangerous. They had witnessed the German captain shooting a fellow Italian soldier when the man had asked to clarify his instructions. The incident made Calogero and Pietro more determined to blow up a railroad bridge that had been used to bring German tanks and other equipment to the Italian troops. Pietro laughed as he described how they feigned no knowledge when questioned by the German officer. They pretended they did not understand his German-Italian. They described other times when they frustrated the Germans' plans by pretending to be stupid, convinced that by this action they were bringing the war closer to its end. When word came that the American and British armies were within sight of capturing the German and Italian soldiers they stepped up their secretive missions. Eager to surrender, they surprised their captors by welcoming them.

I could appreciate how proud and respectful Dino and Maria were of their father and uncle as I, too, was in awe of the risks they took as part of the resistance movement.

I had made arrangements at the Ecumenical Institute to meet one of my classmates who was studying at the North American Pontifical College in Rome. He had agreed to act as tour guide for my father and me around Rome and the Vatican. First, I had to convince my father not to challenge Father Lawrence on theological or biblical issues, as I knew he liked to do. He agreed to ask questions only about landmarks. I kept my fingers crossed, knowing how difficult it would be for my father not to engage in an argument.

To my surprise, he did not challenge anything Father Larry said about the Pope, the Catholic Church, or the Vatican. However, in the evening when Dad and I were having dinner, he couldn't hold back.

"Yes, St. Peter's was beautiful, especially the Pieta, but was all that gold necessary when there are so many poor people in the world? Why do they have these foolish rules to force you to cover your arms before you went inside the church? It's such a hot day, it does not make sense in this day and age to require covering your arms and head!"

I agreed with him, but shrugged my shoulders, trying to calm his ranting.

As Dad promised, on Sunday we visited the Waldensian church in Rome and sang familiar hymns in Italian. Both Dad and I were warmly welcomed, and one family insisted we have Sunday *pronza*, Sunday lunch, with them. The single man in the family, Costantino, was eager to show me Rome and to take me wherever I wanted to go. He told me he wanted to move to America, a red flag that put me off. I was not about to become someone's passport to the USA. My father and I agreed to be taken to visit the Waldensian Seminary and two protestant bookshops. After having *granita*, a cooling lemon ice, my Dad and I bid them farewell.

Because I had already driven twenty-two hundred miles, I was hoping we could take the ferry from Naples to Palermo in Sicily. However, when we inquired about the cost, Dad said it was prohibitive. It was the equivalent of fifty dollars for the car and another fifty for my Dad and me —one way! Instead, we climbed in the car at eight-thirty in the morning and I continued to drive. The roads were not as good as they were in the northern part of Italy, but Dad insisted we should try to make the ferry that would take us from the mainland to Messina. Once we got to Messina, he urged me to drive on to Canicatti in the south central part of Sicily. I had been driving seventeen hours. We only stopped for one meal the whole day, lunching in the car on bread, cheese, fruit, and bottled water. I was disappointed to learn that not all the petrol stations had restrooms so we were obliged to stop when we found thick bushes and trees along the way. I was doing all the driving with my father urging, "Keep going, we're almost there."

At last, we arrived at one-thirty in the morning. Zia Calogera, my Dad's youngest sister, had a large house with polished marble floors. Dad's bedroom and a large bathroom with a sink and tub were on the second floor along with a closet with a glass door. On the first floor was one large room with a beautiful polished wood dining room table that would seat twelve, and a small day bed where Zia Calogera slept. The kitchen where she cooked and ate was off this large dining and sleeping room. She had prepared a bed for me on the second floor, in the small glassed-in closet. I was so tired I couldn't wait to get into the bed, but she had instructions for me: "You cannot use the bathtub, we have water rationing, no brushing teeth, only flush toilet once a day."

My Dad was standing behind her, and he explained, "The city only allows water on Tuesday and Friday mornings for about an hour and a half each time. It has to be used for cooking, cleaning, and washing clothes. So, no baths!"

I wondered how I would survive for the two weeks visit without a bath, and unable to wash my hair or brush my teeth. I fell into bed and put off such decisions until the next day.

About four-thirty in the morning, I heard voices and a commotion outside the closet where I was sleeping. Four young women were standing outside my door, gazing and talking about me.

"*Que bella dona, Americana, no?*" "What a beautiful American young woman, yes?"

During the two weeks that I visited Zia Calogero, the cousins and their friends came by to view their American cousin each morning before they went to work. Sometimes a new girl appeared to observe me, but most of the time it was the same cousins. I hated waking up every morning to all those eyes peering through the closet door. When I complained to my father, he told me, "They don't mean any harm, they are curious."

I learned to accept these intrusive visits as I got acquainted with some of my younger cousins. One cousin, Mella, explained that they had never seen an American girl, and were curious. Very few homes had television and because most people had seen cowboy movies, they believed all American girls and women looked and dressed like those in the westerns. I laughed when she told me, "We all like the way you dress, not wearing the long dresses we have seen in the movies."

I was surprised with how much they did not know, but pleased they approved of my attire.

Mella was a very attractive young woman in her early twenties with a fiancé living in Zurich. I learned that many young men found jobs in Switzerland and Germany since there were no jobs in Canicatti, the same way it was when my father had left more than fifty years earlier. The young men were not allowed to become citizens of those countries, but they did not mind because they did not want to be Germans or Swiss. They were loyal to Italy and returned to Sicily for holidays and vacations. Mella said that she hoped to marry the following year when her fiancé would have saved enough money for her to move to Zurich. For the present, she worked in the fields. He lived with her brother while they both worked in a factory, sharing a flat with two other young men from Canicatti. Mella insisted I meet these fellows when I returned to Switzerland following my father's departure for the states. She said she would write them to arrange our meeting.

While we were in Canicatti, Calogero and Margherita came to Sicily from Montecatini for a visit. We arranged to pack a picnic lunch, and drove to Agrigento where Calogero and my father visited another one of my aunts, who was in the mental hospital in Agrigento. After their visit, the four of us wandered up and down the huge steps of one of the many Greek temples, and had our picnic lunch sitting on the large roots of an ancient olive tree. Calogero told me that there were more Greek temples standing in this part of Sicily than in Greece.

I loved being in Agrigento with Calogero, Margherita, and my father and hearing some of the stories of the Greek temples there.

I asked, "Does that mean that we might have Greek ancestors?"

"Of course," Calogero replied. Many Sicilians have Greek, Spanish, French, Moroccan and even British blood, since Sicily was conquered by all those countries over the last two thousand years.

Wow, this was information my Dad had never told me. I was fascinated by how much I hadn't learned from my history classes in high school and college. I remembered that my Dad had only a third grade education, so this was new for him, too.

Although I did not spend much time with Zia Filomena, I really liked her. She apologized for not remembering any English from her stay in New York. She was tiny with gray hair neatly pulled back in a bun. She laughed easily and conveyed warmth I had not seen in Zia Calogera. She dressed in black, as did most women in Italy her age. The custom was to wear black for a year to mourn the loss of a close relative.

Zia Filomena had a small black and white television and often invited her neighbors to watch with her. She talked fondly about her three years in New York City when she worked as a seamstress. She showed me the Singer sewing machine she brought back with her, which had provided her with a living in Canicatti. Filomena said she had no need to marry since she supported herself and, besides, most of the eligible young men had died in the war. She pointed out that her sister, Calogera, lost her husband in the war and although she had a son, he was a ne'er do well, only interested in traveling around in his Vespa. I had a good feeling about Zia Filomena, impressed with how content she was with her life.

My father introduced me to his two closest friends in Canicatti, Dr. and Mrs. Greco. They were a charming older couple and they spoke English. As we sat around the dining room table enjoying a delicious lunch which Mrs. Greco had prepared from vegetables from her own garden, they told me how they came to Canicatti. Dr. Greco had been a dentist in Springfield, Massachusetts and their desire their whole lives was to retire to a small farm near Canicatti, where he had grown up. I was amazed to learn that the Grecos had become protestants in New England and now they were working with my father to start a small protestant church in Canicatti. The previous year, Dad had written me requesting money for hymn books and bibles. I had made a small contribution to his project, but I had not thought much about what he was doing. I met others who enthusiastically attended the bible study group and hymn sing on Sunday afternoons. The Grecos and Dad were careful not to compete with the local catholic church by avoiding having meetings on Sunday mornings. The Grecos praised my Dad for his energy in recruiting people to the group and his knowledge of the Bible. They said they were going to miss Dad when he returned to New York to visit my sisters and brothers for the summer. Dad assured them that he would return before winter arrived in upstate New York, and would bring money he hoped to raise from visits to American churches.

This was a side of my father that I had not seen before. He had found something close to his heart that he could throw himself into. I was pleased that he was committed to teaching the local people the Bible, introducing his favorite hymns to them and I hoped he was not alienating the local parish priest, which surely would get him into trouble. It reassured me to learn Dad was on good terms with the priest and that they'd had frequent discussions about Bible passages. The priest was surprised at my father's extensive biblical knowledge.

After two weeks in Canicattì, with Zia Calogera making nasty remarks about my being a *prima donna,* it was time to leave. She complained that I raised too many questions about whether fruits, vegetables, and coffee were clean. There were times when I removed a fly from my coffee and still drank it for I knew she would have made a fuss if I'd mentioned it. We had arguments about men going to the moon. Zia Calogera insisted the earth was flat and believed it was impossible for men to go to the moon. My father reminded me that she had not had an education and it was useless to try to convince her the earth was not flat.

The morning that Dad and I were to leave, as we began packing the car with our luggage, cousins arrived with gifts of baked goods for our journey. I thought, here we go again. It was more food than any two people could eat, but we had to accept it to show our appreciation. At least six cousins were bearing gifts, but fortunately there were no bottles of homemade wine!

This time, we took the overnight ferry from Palermo to Naples and I delivered my Dad to the Fumicino airport in Rome, where he caught his flight to the states. I traveled on to Montecatini to spend a few days with (by now) my favorite cousins, Calogero, Margherita and their two children Maria and Dino. We spent more relaxed time in Florence, Lucca, and La Spezia, where cousin Pietro and his family lived and had their pizza restaurant by the sea. I reluctantly left Montecatini, determined to return someday.

For the next three months, I traveled first to Zurich staying with my young male cousin and his friends, as I had promised Mella, then on to France, Belgium, the Netherlands, staying with friends along the way. Finally, I took the ferry to England, where I visited my friend Barbara, near York, and Richard, a young anglican priest, who had been one of my classmates at the Ecumenical Institute. His parents lived near London and welcomed me warmly. (I learned years later that they were hoping their son would ask me to marry.) Richard gave me an insiders's guide to London, with so much history I could barely grasp it all. He introduced me to the National Gallery, where we spent several hours digesting six hundred years of art. When he realized how much I appreciated the collection, he urged me to drive north to Scotland, which I had always thought of as my spiritual home, since presbyterians trace our heritage to Scotland. He said the National Gallery of Scotland was quite small compared to the London Gallery, but that it had some unusually fine exhibits. He thought I would enjoy seeing the painting of a minister skating on a pond. I followed his advice and ended up buying a print of that painting.

I did not have friends in Scotland, but soon found a wonderful bed and breakfast overlooking Inverness. It had been a large manor house with servants' quarters. The owners had recently begun to take in a few guests. The only other guest while I was there was an English businessman. We had dinner together and, over coffee in front of the fireplace in the lounge, he complimented me, saying he had never met an American that wasn't arrogant until he met me. I assured him that there were many Americans who were not overbearing and who were eager to learn about other countries. He still insisted he had not met one!

When I went to my room, I discovered that a hot water bottle had been placed in the bed. At first I did not think I would need it, but discovered its importance when the house became extremely cold. It was much colder in Scotland in July than at home in New York State.

By now, I began to think about returning home. I was missing my sisters, brothers, and friends, and was looking forward to starting my new job. I returned to Paris to turn in the Simca. It still smelled of wine, but fortunately I was not penalized.

My five-month adventure in Europe had been life changing. It made me proud to see a new side of my father, who was starting a small church in his hometown. I met hundreds of relatives I had not known before, and learned to value my Italian heritage and culture. Many new friends from the Ecumenical Institute whom I visited throughout Europe showed me how they lived simply and without pretense. I had a growing appreciation of art, history, music, and the beauty of gardens. The grandeur of the great cathedrals and even the smallest churches throughout the British Isles and the continent captivated me. My life felt fuller, and I was eager to share my experiences with my sisters and brothers back in the States. I was determined to help them take a similar European journey. I wanted them to feel as connected to our Italian relatives and culture as I did.

CHAPTER FIFTEEN

ACCEPTANCE

*D*uring 1964 and 1965, the civil rights movement continued to capture the attention of our nation. I decided I needed to do my part. In July of 1965 during my summer vacation I travelled to Mississippi and volunteered in the Voter Registration Project in the Delta area. For my housing, I contributed a few dollars a day to an African-American family in Greenville, in return for breakfast and a bed in their humble home. Looking around at the sparsely furnished rooms, I could see how much they might appreciate those few extra dollars.

We volunteers gathered in a small church for the orientation. There were about fifteen of us, mostly young men and women who had come from various parts of the North ready to do whatever was needed in the voter registration drive. During the orientation, the project director, a tall black man in his mid-thirties, warned all of us volunteers that FBI men were roaming the streets and taking photos of whites in the African-American neighborhoods. He said in addition to possible harassment by the FBI, we were potential targets for the young Ku Klux Klansmen, who had been responsible for murdering a number of volunteers from the North. He warned us it could be dangerous just walking the streets, we should venture out only in groups, and not go anywhere alone. I understood the danger, but I was unafraid and determined to make a difference in this important project.

Until 1964, the state of Mississippi had required a "poll tax" before anyone could register. Poor people, especially blacks who could not afford the tax, were denied the vote. As part of the registration process, once the tax was paid, the registrar would ask questions of the person applying to register. The questions that the white citizens were asked were very easy but the ones asked of the Negroes were deliberately inscrutable or irrelevant. Our task as volunteers in the Voter Registration Project was to explain to the residents the January 1964 change in the federal law. It eliminated the poll tax for federal elections. Now, any citizen could freely register for national elections, but the law did not apply to voting at the local and state level. The confusion over these details led to most people's reluctance to even attempt to register.

I was not used to the extreme heat and humidity of Mississippi. With my sweaty clothes dripping, I walked the streets talking with those I met (mostly unemployed men) about their new voting rights. When I told them enthusiastically that "times are changing," most of them were not impressed. They didn't believe their state would abide by the new law.

Some folks we encountered told us stories about people they knew who had tried to pay the poll tax in the past, but they still had been denied registration and voting privileges. One older black man said that years ago white local government workers had humiliated, rejected, and even shot at his father to discourage him from even attempting to register. Most of the people we encountered assured me they had given up the idea of voting long ago. When I heard their stories, I realized what a tough assignment we had. People were not convinced that times were indeed changing in Mississippi, and they were confused by the differences between the federal and state laws. Still, I tried to convince those we encountered on the street, and even offered to accompany them to the county clerk's office to assist them in registering. There were very few takers.

My other assignment was to inform the black residents of Greenville, Mississippi about a new federal program for preschool children called "Head Start." We went door to door where we found mothers and grandmothers who were more cordial than the men we'd met on the street. They didn't always invite us in, but most of the time they listened intently. Often they smiled when we introduced ourselves, and most of the women were keenly interested in better educational opportunities for their children. They asked questions about how much it would cost, and even asked whether the teachers were going to be from out of town.

Some were skeptical about a new program that was free, but they wanted to learn all they could because they were eager for their children to have a better education than they had.

We noticed men in unmarked cars with small cameras sticking out the windows roaming the streets and snapping photos of us volunteers. I wondered if they were the FBI or the KKK. We all worried that we would be put in an FBI file and afraid the KKK might use our photos to intimidate and harass us. We all knew about Mrs. Viola Liuzzo, a Detroit housewife, who had been ambushed and murdered by the Klan earlier that year as she was transporting marchers in her car. The project director told us to be watchful and to avoid congregating in a way that might increase the suspicion of the FBI or provide the KKK with a situation they could take advantage of, as they had with Mrs. Liuzzo. So many other civil rights volunteers throughout the south had lost their lives since 1955, the time of the first voter registration drive. We were right to be cautious.

One evening that summer a group of white volunteers and young African-Americans together were invited to the home of the progressive Greenville newspaper publisher, Hodding Carter, III. He had become owner of the paper at a very young age, succeeding his father. Carter delighted in having a mixed group swimming in his private pool. He proudly told us that it was probably the only pool in Mississippi where a mixed group could swim. I was pleased to hear Hodding Carter, the third, talk about his commitment to civil rights in spite of the dangers from the Ku Klux Klan. He said times were changing and Mississippi needed to change, too. It was time to support the civil rights of all Americans. Carter and his newspaper received a number of awards for their courageous stand.

On most nights we gathered in one of the small African-American churches, where we listened to local leaders talk about the problems they faced. We heard about those who had given their lives for the cause of freedom, like Mrs. Liuzzo. The local leaders told us how much they appreciated help from those of us who had come from the North.

"We couldn't do this without you," they assured us.

One night we were told that Fannie Lou Hamer was coming to speak to us. We sang spirituals and freedom songs as we waited for this famous woman to arrive. As she hobbled in, I was amazed that in spite of her physical disabilities and obvious pain she continued to devote her life to "the cause." She had been injured during a civil rights march, and had been jailed and abused by the police. She was poor, with a limited education, but despite this she had organized and challenged men and women throughout the South to become involved in some aspect of the civil rights movement in their own communities. I was thrilled to listen to and meet this legendary figure of the movement. No one could sit still when Fannie Lou spoke about the injustices: the poor education of blacks throughout the South, the lack of adequate medical care, and the inability to vote, which was the basic right of all Americans. She would burst into song, and we all would rise and join in singing hymns, spirituals, and freedom songs. These evenings always ended with holding hands and singing "We Shall Overcome." When we sang "Black and White Together", we swayed back and forth, many of us moved to tears. I thought how strong our country would be if we truly were together without the racial divisions that separate us. These gatherings helped us keep our focus and our determination, in spite of our weariness after long and often discouraging days.

One evening Danny, the fifteen-year-old son of the family where I was staying, injured his leg while he was chopping wood for his family. It looked to me like he had broken it, and he was in pain. Since I was not a doctor, I gently suggested he needed to go to the hospital. The parents glanced at each other and told me, "Naw, he won't be treated and we don't have a way to get there. He be all right."

"What if I took him to the emergency room? Would that help?"

They shook their heads, "He might not be admitted to the emergency room. Besides it would be a very long wait." The parents looked at each other, as if to reconsider. His mother said, "Maybe with a white woman by his side he might have a better chance."

They were right. After two hours of waiting, watching other white patients being treated ahead of us, I finally spoke up and managed to get a nurse to attend to the boy. Indeed he had broken his leg, and the emergency room doctor proceeded to immobilize his leg with a cast. He might have spent the rest of his life limping with a damaged leg, had I not taken him to the hospital.

I was seeing first-hand how Mississippi treated black people. This experience convinced me of the need to change not only the laws, but the attitudes and behavior of the white community.

I worked in Mississippi for only part of that summer, but it was an experience that opened my eyes to injustices that had prevailed for many years. I remembered how my father had been treated with disdain because he spoke broken English. He'd been told "go back to the old country, you Wop!" My father and his Italian-American friends were made to feel inferior and had been treated as second class citizens, too. Inspired by the bus boycott started by Rosa Parks in Montgomery, Alabama, by Fannie Lou Hamer, Dr. Martin Luther King, and my seminary friend, Reverend Andrew Young, I was determined to find a way to continue my involvement in the civil rights movement. I did not know where or how, only that I would find a way to work to improve the conditions of people of color as well as others treated as inferior.

I returned to my job at the end of the summer, continuing my work with the presbyterian churches in Pennsylvania, West Virginia, and Kentucky. I discovered my Mississippi experience had changed me. I was emboldened to challenge those church people who expressed intolerance of what was happening in the South. At a teacher's meeting in western Pennsylvania, when I heard some of the women condemning those who went South referring to them as "trouble makers," I introduced myself as one of the "trouble makers." I could see their surprise and embarrassment, but I went on to describe my experience in Mississippi. I asked how many of them would be willing to pay money to vote. Then I told them about some of the black citizens I had met who had been denied the vote because they could not pay the poll tax. I described my experience at the emergency room of the hospital in Greenville. They listened silently. I challenged them to consider what life would be like in western Pennsylvania if they were living in similar conditions to those I described in Mississippi. After the meeting, three of the teachers said that before hearing me, they had not really believed the stories they had heard. The pictures on the television confirmed their mistaken beliefs that it was the trouble makers who were responsible for the problems. After listening to a first-hand report from me, they began to understand and appreciate the problems that intolerance had caused black people for so many years.

Despite these successes, I grew tired of living out of a suitcase and traveling to a different location every two weeks. Without a home, it was difficult to develop long-lasting friendships. I began to desire a new life where I would be able to put down some roots and have a home again, with my own things around me. I applied for and was offered two positions as Director of Christian Education. One was in Grosse Point, Michigan and the other in Brooklyn, New York. Although the Grosse Point position would pay more, as a city girl I was in love with New York, and opted for the Brooklyn job. The mixture of races was a factor in my decision, thanks to my Mississippi experience.

I would be working with three churches in Brooklyn. It would be quite a challenge, since the only thing they had in common besides being presbyterian was that they were on the same subway line. One church was a Puerto Rican congregation of recent arrivals, with a white single pastor who had learned Spanish in order to serve his people. Another was a combination of Koreans and African-Americans with another white single minister who was helping both ethnic groups understand and appreciate each other's culture. This was unusual in the sixties. The Korean and African-Americans had separate services in their own language, but had gradually begun to worship together. This church prided itself in having the poet Marianne Moore as an active member.

The third was what I called "Wall Street White." The First Presbyterian Church of Brooklyn was close to Wall Street and the Brooklyn Bridge. The congregation represented the wealth of Wall Street and the Brooklyn Heights area. It prided itself in having not only brokers, but actors who starred in popular TV soaps and on Broadway. This church provided me with a one-bedroom apartment in the brownstone next door to the church. It was an ideal location, convenient to the subway and the shops of downtown Brooklyn, and I would not need a car.

The minister of the church was married and lived on the first two floors with his family. My three-room apartment was on the third floor. I was excited about having a professional position and an apartment in the city I loved.

In my new job I planned to do an assessment of the educational level of the teachers and how they used the presbyterian curriculum of Bible-based moral and ethical lessons. I was keen to train the teachers of the three churches to the level of competency of public school teachers, as I had done in Watertown and Youngstown. According to the three pastors, the teachers were open to any training I might offer. When I began visiting the classes on Sunday in the First Presbyterian Church of Brooklyn, I was surprised to discover they paid their Sunday school teachers. I had never heard of a church that paid its teachers. Perhaps because most of them were professionally trained, and with the church's links to Wall Street, it could afford to pay them. Two of the teachers were already ordained ministers, and were completing advanced degrees at Union Theological Seminary in Manhattan.

Archie, a popular teacher of the senior high class, was handsome and soft spoken, a young African-American student at Union Seminary. I had met him briefly the previous January when I had come to the church for my job interview. He was finishing his Master's degree in psychiatry and religion. I was impressed by what he was studying and his previous experience as a Chaplain Intern at San Quentin prison and at a medical center in Detroit. He told me he had been working at the prison at Riker's Island, as well as at the Rusk Institute (a rehabilitation hospital for spine chord injuries), Goldwater Memorial hospital, and Bellevue's psychiatric facility.

The minister of the church gave Archie a key to the church and permission to use the electric typewriter to complete his final papers before graduating. In a city where the custom was to have several locks on doors to prevent burglaries, I realized the high level of trust they had in him. From my living room I could see the church office, and noticed that the light was on long into the night. On evenings when he saw the lights on in my apartment, he began to phone me. Often he could hear the music I was playing and would comment on how much he liked my selections. We compared our musical preferences and discovered that we had similar interests. We both loved jazz and choral church music. He had sung in his college *acapella* choir at Linfield College in McMinnville, Oregon, as I had in Wooster.

Each Sunday I began to observe the classes to assess what kind of training was needed. In my attempt to be inconspicuous and to avoid disturbing the class, I would tip-toe in and out of each classroom. The one time I visited Archie's senior high class he was drawing a diagram on the blackboard describing the Freudian theory of the id, the ego, and the superego. Because I knew he would be graduating and gone soon, I decided it was not necessary to spend much time observing him. I silently began to leave the room. However, he interrupted his lecture, pointed to me, and said, "I'm going to get to Jesus Christ in a minute."

Attempting to be unobtrusive, I smiled and continued to slip out of the room. After church that Sunday, he asked me to have lunch with him in a nearby restaurant. I suspected that he felt I had judged him, and that his invitation to lunch was to justify what he was teaching. I was right.

After ordering lunch, he frowned and said, "You left my classroom too soon. I was going to get to Jesus, but I wanted to make a point using Freud's theory of the self."

"You don't have to explain," I said. "I was not judging you. Using the illustration of the self made perfect sense to me. I just needed to observe some of the other classrooms to assess what training is needed. Since you will be leaving soon, it did not seem necessary for me to spend much time in your classroom."

His face relaxed. He smiled and said, "That's a relief. I thought you would give me a negative report."

We lingered over lunch, telling each other about our families, college, and our seminary experiences. We both loved living in Brooklyn. I told him about my work in the voter registration project in Mississippi and he talked of his hopes for his new job in Massachusetts, to start in three weeks.

The next week, he and his roommate, a fellow student at Union, invited me to a dinner they had prepared, and I in turn invited them to my apartment for an Italian meal.

Archie told me, "I'm sorry there is so little time to show you my favorite jazz places in the Village. Maybe on a day off, I can come back to the city and take you to some clubs."

I did not take his offer seriously. I thought when he got to Worcester he would have many demands in his new job and would develop other interests. I considered our conversations pleasant and friendly, but nothing else.

Our friendship continued another two weeks until he asked me to attend his graduation from Union Seminary, to be held at Riverside Church. I did go to Riverside, but did not see him afterward because of the huge crowd. The next day I learned from his roommate, Archie had already left New York for his new job in Massachusetts. There were no good-byes, but I was intrigued when he called me and apologized for not seeing me before he moved. He then began calling me almost every night, reading his sermons and asking for my thoughts and suggestions. I was flattered that he wanted my input. He told me about his new position in Worcester as Minister to the Community. His task was to get a foothold into the non-white, non-church community and begin to develop some relationships in order to determine what programs he might start. I began to look forward to his calls to hear about his experiences and the challenges he was facing. Occasionally I made suggestions. When he didn't call me, I was disappointed.

Our phone conversations grew longer and more frequent. During one call he told me he was surprised that I had been to Europe, but never to the West Coast. He said, "I'm planning to go to Seattle for the Fourth of July weekend to officiate at my sister Joyce's wedding. Why don't you go with me? This would be a good chance for you to see the Pacific Northwest."

I was reluctant, "I have tentative plans to meet my friend, Bill, the Canadian Air Force officer, but I will think about your invitation. I'd like to see Seattle."

While traveling in England during the summer of 1964, I'd met Bill, a lieutenant in the Canadian Air Force, whom I had begun seeing on our return to North America. I had told Archie about Bill and my misgivings about the relationship, which had been psychologically abusive at times. On the phone that night, Archie convinced me that it was time to break off with Bill and travel to Seattle with him. I knew he was right. I did need to end things with Bill and the next day I wrote the "dear john" letter that ended the relationship. When I reported my decision to

Archie, he was delighted and said, "Well done!"

I looked forward to the trip with Archie. On the airplane, he told me more about his family, how his grandparents had moved to Seattle from Mississippi when they were in their mid-seventies. They had bought a small house across the street from Archie's parents, and as he grew up, he became very close to them. He talked about what he wanted me to see.

"From the dining room window of my family's home, we can see Mount Rainier. It is awesome, not like those hills that you call Catskill Mountains," he teased.

When I was introduced to his three sisters and brother, he noted that one of his sisters and I looked very much alike—petite, with similar skin coloring and hairstyle. They all were down-to-earth, and made me feel comfortable by letting me help in the kitchen with meal preparation, setting the table, and other tasks related to the wedding. I was careful to ask his older sister, Marge, for directions on how to cut the vegetables or prepare the punch. I thought of myself as a good cook, but I did not want to inadvertently offend anyone by taking the initiative to do things "my way."

Archie's father was a large man with a captivating smile who took pride in showing me his vegetable garden. His love of gardening reminded me of my own father. He was interested in hearing about my Dad's success with growing vegetables, and he commented that it must be more difficult planting in northern New York where there was so much snow and such frigid temperatures. He told me it was not that cold nor was there much snow in Seattle, which surprised me. He told me the Seattle rains were especially good for planting collard greens, swiss chard, potatoes, tomatoes, peppers and for the blackberry bushes in their yard. I thought my father and Archie's dad would have lots to share.

His mother was a beautiful woman with high cheek bones that signified her mixed ancestry of Native American and African-American. Archie had told me how industrious she was, how she had helped her two sons go to college by cleaning houses during the day and working eight hours until midnight cleaning an office building. Everyone in the family seemed to take pride in their appearance. I thought they could have walked out of a fashion magazine.

On Sunday I was expected to attend church with Archie's grandmother. His sisters tried to prepare me for her outbursts of "thank you, Jesus." I was familiar with the exchange between preacher and congregation from my experience in Mississippi and other black churches, but I was still surprised when she frequently punctuated the preacher's sermon with "yes, Lord" and "Thank you, Jesus." It was obvious that the whole family, the congregation, and the preacher were used to Grandma Callie's enthusiastic shouts. When she started singing, the congregation joined in. Archie said she felt the "Spirit" leading her. The hymns were the same ones sung in Italian in my parents' pentecostal church. Although it was a baptist church rather than a presbyterian one, I felt at home.

After the service, Archie introduced me to his beloved pastor and made a point of telling him of my work in Christian education and my time in Mississippi. I noticed that it seemed important to Archie to have his pastor's approval of me. At that time I did not realize how significant that was.

His parents, brother and sisters were warm and included me as if I were a member of the family. I really liked them all, especially his Mississippi-born grandmother and grandfather who were in their eighties.

On the red eye flight back to New York City Archie leaned over, took my hand and said, "I want to marry you!"

I was surprised and speechless for a few minutes. "Are you sure you want to marry me? Maybe we should think about it."

He laughed, "I am sure, and I know you are, too."

I began to realize that we had fallen in love, and that his invitation to Seattle was to get his family's and his pastor's approval of me. Although we had known each other for only two months, we both recognized that we had grown in our love and respect for each other. We were ready to make a commitment to spend the rest of our lives together. As he had in the past, he assured me that he had been impressed with my strength of character, especially as he came to understand how I had kept my family together and raised some of my sisters and brothers. He reminded me that he'd had numerous girl friends but none of them had been strong women, which he said was what attracted him to me.

161

Neither of us could have imagined what was in store for us when we arrived in New York.

After traveling all night on the plane, we were bleary-eyed when we arrived at my apartment. I unlocked the door, and as I entered, I immediately sensed something was not right. A man's shirt hung on the back of the sofa, and another one on the back of a chair. I looked into my bedroom and someone—a man—was in my bed.

I turned to Archie, who was bringing the luggage up the stairs, and said, "Someone's in my apartment!"

I was frightened. I couldn't understand how someone, obviously, a man, could be in my apartment.

He said, "Don't go in there, we'll call the police."

We were both puzzled. Then I saw my father getting out of my bed! I turned to Archie, "It's okay, it's my father!"

He asked, "I thought your Dad was in Italy?"

"I did, too. I have no idea how he got to New York and into my apartment."

When Dad had dressed he came out and wanted to know where I had been, and who was this black man I was with. First, I wanted to know how he had gotten into my apartment. He said when he arrived from Italy and couldn't find me home, he convinced the building superintendent to let him into my apartment. He said he told the super "maybe she's just gone for the day." But he had been waiting for me for three days.

"Why didn't you write to tell me when you were coming?"

"I thought you would be here," he said.

I introduced him to Archie, who stood in the living room surrounded by the luggage.

"Daddy, I am going to marry Archie."

The raging storm began! Dad yelled, in Italian, "No! You can't. It's not possible to marry a man who isn't white."

I felt my stomach doing somersaults. I thought, here we go again. I retorted, "What do you mean, it's not possible? There is no law that says we can't marry!"

"Cats and dogs don't mate! It's not God's plan for whites and Negroes to marry."

I said, "Where does the Bible say that?" Of course, he was stumped. He repeated the cats and dogs argument. After that he spent the next several hours talking with me in Italian. The truth was he was yelling at me, demanding I change my mind. He asked again whether I had lost my mind. I thought, I can't believe this is happening!

I worried about Archie's feelings. Although he could not understand everything my father was saying, he certainly could catch the angry tone, my father's head and hands shaking as he yelled at me. I tried to calm my father, at the same time trying to reassure Archie that we'd get through this tirade.

I tried to prepare some breakfast for Archie and me, but he decided it was time for him to leave. He said he needed to drive to his new job in Worcester. I could appreciate how uncomfortable it was for him to see the way my father was carrying on. I was reluctant to see him reach for the door, leaving me alone to struggle with my father. As in the past, I was more determined than ever to make my own decisions, and would not allow my father to interfere with my plans.

As Archie was leaving I said, "I will call you this evening."

What a homecoming it had been. Instead of being happy about getting married, I found myself in another battle with my father.

That evening after my father had gone to bed, Archie and I talked by phone.

He said, "I told you how painful it was when I was rejected a few years ago by the parents of the girl I wanted to marry." I remembered what Archie had told me about that awful experience.

I assured him, "That will not happen this time. I will not allow my father to stand in our way. He can be very difficult but we will work things out. I have had to fight battles with him in the past and I will not be deterred by his ignorance."

Archie told me, "One of the things that has drawn me to you is your strength. If anyone can convince your Dad, you can."

Archie had given me the vote of confidence I needed to stay firm in my decision to marry him.

Dad stayed with me a few days and then traveled to a Rochester suburb in upstate New York where he planned to spend the summer with Rosalie, her husband, Bob, and their two sons. Before he left, he passionately tried to persuade me again to change my plans. I was unrelenting in my determination to marry the man I believed that God had chosen for me.

The next month, in August of 1966, Archie was invited to preach in the all-white baptist church in Rochester where he had done his field work and where he was much loved. He invited me to accompany him. My father was living close to Rochester, and I saw this as an opportunity to have my father see Archie in his role as a minister. I invited my Dad to come to the church to hear Archie preach. Knowing my father's religious fervor, I was sure this would have a favorable impact on him. Following the service, my father told me he was quite impressed with the warm response by the parishioners to Archie. They hugged and kissed him and the parents of the young people who had been in Archie's youth group told me what a positive influence Archie had been on their children. They missed him and wished they could have him back, but they knew he was now one of the ministers of a large baptist church in Massachusetts.

That clinched it for Dad. He did an about-face, and not only accepted Archie, but offered to pay for a family dinner in a restaurant the evening before our wedding. I couldn't believe my ears! Seeing Archie as a minister made all the difference to my father. He was finally able to accept and embrace Archie as a future son-in-law.

CHAPTER SIXTEEN

TOGETHER

We decided we wanted a small wedding to be held in the chapel at Colgate Rochester Divinity School where Archie had gone to seminary, and would invite only family and close friends. This was not to be a big expensive affair. I asked a friend to make a simple yellow street-length dress for me and Archie wore a suit. My sister, Doris, agreed to be my maid-of-honor and Archie's childhood friend, John, was his best man. One of Archie's seminary professors whom we both admired would perform the brief ceremony in September of 1966 in Rochester.

I did not want my father to accompany me down the aisle so Archie and I walked together with Doris and John ahead of us. Although our relationship had developed quickly, I felt that somehow we could make it a successful marriage as long as we worked together.

My sisters, brothers, nieces, nephews, Aunt Fay, a few close friends and my father were present. Archie's mother was there, too, the only one from his family who could make the long trip from Seattle. She was beautifully attired, her face reflecting her happiness and pride in our wedding. The previous evening I had recognized how my father was quite taken by her beauty and grace. Archie had invited a few close friends from the church where he had worked when he was a student. I was pleased that we were having the simple wedding that we had planned together.

As we walked down the aisle Archie squeezed my hand. I suddenly realized how unexpected it was that I should marry, and yet here I was, walking down the aisle with a man I'd known only four and a half months. I had butterflies in my stomach with the excitement of it and yet I knew deep in my heart that we had made the right decision; we would have a successful marriage working together for what we believed in so passionately. I remember his smile as he squeezed my hand again and leaned over to kiss me. How happy I was!

After the wedding Archie's mother hugged me and told me that it was her birthday. She said our wedding was the best birthday present she could have. I was pleased that Archie's mother had embraced me so warmly. My father surprised me when he told her what a blessing her son was. Archie gave me his look of assurance that he had finally made it with my father. I, too, had finally made peace with my Dad after so many battles over the years and on my wedding day!

Archie and I were thrilled that we had support from those we loved. This would help us ignore those who had warned us it would be impossible to have a stable inter-racial marriage during this period of unrest at the height of the civil rights struggle in our country.

As I looked around at the loved ones gathered with us, I had a feeling of peace and joy. I knew we were blessed and supported by those who knew and loved us. I knew it was a moment of grace.

I continued to work with the same three churches in Brooklyn for the month of September to prepare them for the beginning of the church school year and then I moved to Worcester, Massachusetts to join my new husband. I hunted for a position as a Director of Christian Education in a presbyterian church but nothing was available.

I began looking for a place for us to live. However, when Archie went with me, the managers would tell us the apartment was no longer available. I became very discouraged and frustrated. We realized we were experiencing first-hand the housing discrimination the civil rights movement was working to change. After about two months and ten rejections, I was afraid we would never find a satisfactory place to live.

Our current housing situation was appalling. We were living in Archie's three-room apartment in what was considered the ghetto of Worcester. Mice and rats would wake us as they scampered along the other side of the walls. I hated to take a bath—spiders and roaches would join me. When televisions were turned on in the evenings, all the lights in the building would go out. We could hear shouting from one family to the next about whose fault it was that the fuse was blown and the electricity out again.

Several members of the church who had helped to furnish Archie's apartment were eager for him to move his bride out of that neighborhood, but no one appreciated the difficulty of finding decent housing nor were they willing to admit to housing discrimination in Worcester.

Finally, a physician who was a member of the church, remembered that his parents' home was still vacant and available. The house was connected to a group of doctors' offices. They had to be cautious about who could be allowed to live in the home, because the doctors kept drugs in their offices. Dr. Ward, the president of First Baptist Church, Archie's employer, offered the seven room house to us for very low rent. We both were elated to finally have a comfortable home conveniently located. We could not have anticipated that the five doctors who took us under their wings would also give us free medical care during the nine years we lived there. It proved to be a wonderful home where we had frequent visits from both of our families and from many friends.

Our marriage proved to be very different from either of our parents' relationships. My father had ruled in his marriage; Archie's mother seemed to have more control in hers. In our relationship we were making decisions together. We did our best each day remembering the advice the minister gave us at the time of our wedding to "take care of each other." This advice also led us to preserve our day off to take care of our relationship.

I helped Archie with his work as Minister to the Community (the poor black, white and Hispanic people of Worcester). We started a bacon-and-egg club that made it possible for people to purchase directly from a farmer at reduced cost. We organized a group of teens and took them on retreats to a camp outside of Worcester where they explored the out-of-doors for the first time and discussed their concerns and fears about their future: drugs, further education, sex, the police, and the limitations of activities in their neighborhoods.

After several months I was hired to develop a wide variety of services in what was called the anti-poverty program part of Lyndon Johnson's "war on poverty." I developed a neighborhood council, a newsletter, recreation programs, and an after school tutoring program. With cooperation from the school department, the health department and the YWCA I started a school-age mothers program for girls to continue their education when they became pregnant, a parent education group, and a family planning program. With one of the psychiatrists from the state hospital I started the first community mental health center. We were addressing a wide variety of the needs of the poorest people in the city. Often Archie and I worked with the same families in our different capacities.

The people of First Baptist Church were successful in finding jobs for some of the former inmates that Archie was supporting as they readjusted to society. The police department, social services, the juvenile court judge and probation officers were eager to provide their assistance to this new way of addressing the multi-faceted needs of the poorer neighborhoods. Archie and I were developing new programs and I began to cook for more than the two of us, for he often brought young men home for supper.

We both worked hard and were gratified to see the new programs were beginning to improve the lives of the people, especially the youth. We had decided early in our marriage that to preserve our own relationship we needed to carefully protect Monday, our day off, for time together. We began exploring New England, in particular Cape Cod and southern Maine.

There were times when we both experienced high profile attention from the local newspaper and it sometimes caused more problems for us. About a year after moving to Worcester, Archie was accused of fomenting the African-American community to riot. He had delivered a sermon highlighting some of the conditions in Worcester's poorer neighborhoods: inadequate housing, high unemployment, and that these were similar to those which existed in Newark and Detroit that had led to riots in those cities. A reporter misquoted Archie in the newspaper the next morning and some of the youth began saying, "If Reverend Archie says there's going to be a riot, we'll make it happen."

The police chief and the city manager were furious and a series of letters to the editor kept the dialogue going for months. No one bothered to get the truth of what was actually said in the sermon. Archie was fortunate that his boss, Gordon Torgersen, the senior minister of the church, supported him. He interceded with the police chief and the city manager and reassured them that Archie was not inciting riots but working to provide programs to avert them. He told them he had heard the sermon and pointed out that the reporter had misrepresented Archie. The police chief and city manager were reassured, but we learned later that they secretly decided to tap our phone to be certain Archie was not planning a riot.

At other times when civil rights activities were keeping tensions high, Archie would be concerned when he was called to the hospital in the middle of the night. He wondered if he was being called away from our home so that someone could do harm to me or our home. He would drive around the block a couple of times to check on our home before going to the hospital. Paranoia was rampant in the city, so we too had to be extremely cautious.

We both were very visible in the community frequently quoted in the local newspaper. Many people knew who we were. When we were being seated in a restaurant we would overhear people pointing saying, "that's Reverend Smith and his wife." This attention made us quite uncomfortable and we became even more determined to get away on our days off, driving to other parts of New England. We loved each other and the work we were doing, but we knew we had to protect our relationship during those difficult times. Those trips on our day off gave us quiet moments and our strong faith sustained and strengthened our marriage through the nine years of demanding and sometimes difficult days in Worcester.

While still in Worcester, Archie continued his work as a family therapist along with his ministry to the non-church community and sometimes we saw couples together.

It was during this time that Archie began to realize that seminary had trained him to think theologically but it had not trained him to know how to deal with current social problems. He decided to leave his position as Minister to the Community after three years and to work toward a doctorate in social planning at Brandeis University. While still a doctoral student, Clark University invited him to teach part time in the sociology department and Holy Cross College asked him to teach in the theology department and to provide support to the newly arrived Black Students. When he had completed his doctoral degree, he accepted a position to become a professor at Pacific School of Religion, an interdenominational seminary in Berkeley, California where he has taught for over thirty years. He has a license as a pastoral counselor and a California license as a Marriage and Family Therapist and continues to provide therapy in a part-time practice.

After our move to California, I returned to school and studied for another Master's degree, this time in clinical psychology and I became a licensed Marriage and Family Therapist. While I maintained a part-time practice as a therapist, I worked as an Administrator of a number of programs: Director of the University YWCA in Berkeley, where I developed programs including an employment service for students and staff at the University of California. I was appointed Director of a Counseling Center and CEO of the American Red Cross for our county, where I worked closely with a staff of twenty-five and an additional fifty trained volunteers who responded to emergencies such as local house fires and larger disasters including the Loma Prieta Earthquake.

My training experience for the church, developing new programs in a low income racially mixed neighborhood in Worcester, and creating support networks for youth have all contributed to a broader perspective in my therapy practice than attributing problems solely to the individual or family. My experience of growing up in a childrens' home helped to make me keenly sensitive to the critical needs of some families at various stages in their development, especially, when mental illness is a factor. People who have heard our family's story tell me that we would not have the strong family ties had it not been for my persistence in holding the family together by being the story-teller that keeps in touch with each of them.

Yes, I am still the family caretaker. Several sisters and brothers have lived with Archie and me at various times when they were in transition. I continue to keep phone and email contacts with each of them and thereby help them to stay connected with each other.

We continue connections with our Messina relatives in Tuscany where Archie and I have visited many times and where two cousins have visited us during the four years Archie and I lived in London. Recently, Charlotte and her husband, Gordon, went to Tuscany to meet some of our relatives. David and Chase (who used to be called Fran) have each spent brief periods of time there. Our cousins have educated us to appreciate the contributions Italians have made to art, music, literature, architecture, the culinary arts and vinoculture. Two young cousins are involved in the Slow Food movement in Italy.

During our growing up years we resented the stigma of being Italian, especially when people assumed we must be Catholic and that was why we had such a large family. Each of us has had to reassure curious people that though we had Sicilian relatives our family was not related to the mafia. Now as grown-ups with our knowledge and appreciation of the contributions of Italians to the arts and especially to music, we are proud of the richness of our Italian heritage.

LtoR: Chase, David, Vincent, Doris, Ron
Rosalie, Jerry, and Charlotte

CHAPTER SEVENTEEN

WHERE ARE THEY?

ROSALIE

As the oldest children, Rosalie and I had looked after our brothers and sisters when we were young. Not surprisingly, we continued in that role throughout our adult years. Rosalie not only made a home for her husband and two sons, but at times took in Doris, Chase, and our father.

After her divorce, Rosalie's first priority was raising her sons. To support them she taught piano, and because music was so important in her life, she introduced the boys to both piano and violin.

Rosalie had always dreamed of a college education. Finally, in her forties she graduated from a college that gave her credit for her life experience in addition to class work.

Soon after that, Rosalie surprised us all when she announced that she'd been called to the ministry. At first I was not very supportive. I felt she might be neglecting her role as mother to her teenaged sons and wondered if she might be competing with me by going to seminary as I had done. I gradually became less critical and accepted her decision convinced of her sincere call to the ministry and that she was not trying to compete with me.

After three years of seminary at Colgate Rochester Divinity School, she planned her ordination to take place on her fiftieth birthday at the Presbyterian Church in Victor, New York. I was pleased when she asked Archie, my husband, to preach the ordination sermon. Except for Chase (formerly Fran), we all were present for this important event in Rosalie's life including Aunt Fay, who was there to give her blessing. The church was crowded with the people whose lives she had touched as a volunteer in the church for thirty years.

Following her ordination, Rosalie had several ministerial positions in churches in western New York State, Orlando, Florida and at the headquarters of the presbyterian denomination in Louisville, Kentucky. In her national position, she traveled almost fifty per cent of the time. She met with church committees around the country and occasionally overseas.

Because I had also worked at the national level of the presbyterian church, Rosalie and I always had much to talk about and I looked forward to her calls from another hotel in another strange city. I'd listen to her frustrations, and her accomplishments, and I'd remind her that our faith had sustained us throughout our growing-up years and would continue to give us strength. She always expressed her gratitude. "That's what I needed to hear. I knew you would have some words of encouragement, I'm glad I called you. I know I am doing the Lord's work but sometimes it's really hard, flying in and out of airports, staying in lonely hotel rooms, and meeting with a new group of people all the time. I guess I just wanted to hear a familiar voice."

Whenever I asked her about her grandson Allen, she always sounded animated. "He's got the lead in a play and he's only a sophomore! I'm so proud of him, I'm planning to go to a performance in a few weeks and I'm hoping he will go with me this summer to a work camp in Mexico with some high school students from California."

"Gee, Roe, that sounds great, but do you think you will be working too hard? Don't you need a rest?" Her reply was always, "I really want to do something with Allen. He's such a great kid."

Rosalie was an amazing fundraiser. She raised several million dollars from the families of Walmart and Disney for the work of the presbyterian denomination. Rosalie would call me when she had just been promised another million dollars for the work of the church. On a couple of occasions she took me to meet one couple, part of the Disney family, so I could see how much she and her ministry were valued by them. They embraced her warmly as if she was a member of their family and then told me what a terrific minister she was. It seemed important to Rosalie that someone in our family understand the high regard the Disney family had of her especially when she received little recognition from her superiors in the church.

After a memorable trip to New Zealand she considered retiring there but then decided her home was western New York where her two sons and her grandson lived. She said her family was too important for her to live far from them. She visited Archie and me each time we lived in London. The highlight for her was attending the opera with me. We'd dress in our favorite outfits and take the Underground to Covent Garden. She saved her best clothes for these outings. Her hair was still dark, nicely curled and she looked beautiful. We both felt elegant as we found our places in the opera house. On our Underground ride home we discussed the singers, the set, and the opera house. She said she was looking forward to retirement when she planned to go to New York to productions of the Metropolitan Opera. I told her I'd like to go with her someday. Each time she visited us she always included Scotland where she enjoyed a private retreat on the remote Isle of Iona, an ancient presbyterian spiritual site.

Rosalie was an accomplished musician of the piano, cello, and harp, and she hoped to sing in the Eastman Choral Society after retirement. Sadly, at the time of her retirement, she was diagnosed with amyotrophic lateral sclerosis (ALS), also known as Lou Gehrig's disease, which has no cure. It was a devastating blow to her and to all of us. Her sixteen-year-old grandson Allen, moved in and took care of his grandmother that summer, but when he returned to school, she realized she could no longer live alone in her new home. When she moved to a hospice in the Finger Lakes region of New York, our whole family rallied to visit her and provide for her needs to make the end of her life as comfortable as possible. When Chase visited her he discovered she had a craving for lemon ice, an Italian summer delicacy, he scoured the stores in the area until he found some putting a smile on Rosalie's face.

Archie called her every morning to read a psalm and pray with her. She said she looked forward to his phone calls when she woke up each morning. I communicated with her by email until she could no longer use her computer. I hated to see her lose muscle strength, leaving her unable to perform the simplest tasks for herself.

During her last months, friends from all over the country came to visit her and shared stories and reminisced with her. They all told her how much she had meant to them.

Rosalie experienced such anguish when she began to lose her ability to speak. "How can I be a minister and not talk?" I wept as I watched her physical decline, yet she kept her sense of humor. Chase had given Rosalie a small slate board and chalk so she could still communicate after she could no longer speak. Sometimes she would write a silly ditty on it to make us laugh. We always expected humorous birthday cards from her, and it made us sad to know these would end soon.

Her son Bobby moved back to New York State to care for her at the hospice. He fed her and washed her feet to warm them so she could fall asleep at night. Each day he carried her to the car, took her for a drive among the vineyards, and to restaurants on one of the Finger Lakes. We never heard him complain. Rosalie lived in the hospice for five months until she died in July 2003, with her family gathered by her bedside.

She had planned her own funeral and had asked Archie to officiate. Hundreds of people attended and many shared their stories about Rosalie. One young man told how she had twice taken the youth group on 100-mile bike trips through northern New York State. He said they were amazed at her energy as she biked along side the teenagers. Some had taken piano lessons from her and talked of how she was more than their piano teacher, becoming their counselor, listening and guiding them when they were going through difficulties in their family life. Several women told us how she had inspired them to go into the ministry as a second career telling them "it is never too late."

She died two years after her diagnosis, and a year after our mother's death. Her absence was a difficult adjustment for me. I had relied on her to remember incidents and details I had forgotten and had consulted with her frequently as I wrote this memoir. I will always miss Rosalie.

DAVID

David and I have had a special bond, not only because we had both attended the College of Wooster in Ohio, but also because he's the oldest son in our family. There is an unspoken expectation in Italian families that the eldest male has some responsibility for the family when the father is no longer living. All of us look up to David, often consulting with him about areas of his expertise in finance and in pharmaceutical concerns.

During his graduate studies at Ohio State University, he assisted in the laboratory in pancreatic research at the medical school. Then he entered the pharmaceutical field where he excelled in sales and received an *AMA Journal* acknowledgment as one of the top ten pharmaceutical representatives in the nation. For a number of years, David received the highest honors in that field. Eventually he began to look for new life challenges. This led him to the field of financial planning, where again he has been a success.

One time when David was in Syracuse for a family wedding he decided he wanted to visit our mother at Marcy State Hospital. He had not seen her since he was a teenager—in over forty years. Since he was apprehensive about the visit several of us agreed to accompany him. Rosalie had arranged for us to take Mom out to a nearby ice cream shop. When she came to the front door of the state hospital David hurried up the stairs to greet her and before he could introduce himself she said, "Hello, David." We all were amazed that she recognized him after all those years. While we were enjoying our ice cream treats David took Mom's hands and told her, "Your hands are so soft, they are beautiful." She smiled and said, "Your father always used to tell me that." It seemed as if everything was normal and no time had passed. We all were very touched by our mother's remembrances of David and our father.

After a divorce, David moved from Ohio to the Bay area to be closer to Doris, Chase and Archie and me who were already living in northern California. He soon found a position in another pharmaceutical company where he was named West Coast director of managed care and settled into a California lifestyle.

David had enjoyed golf since his early days in Ohio. One afternoon while on a golf course in California he met Lisa (Kim), a Korean-American who had been the owner/chef of a successful French restaurant in San Francisco for twenty years. They married and are very devoted to each other as well as to golf. Since their retirement they have traveled widely to play at various courses, but always return home within a few days to tend to their six birds. Lisa is not only a very successful tournament golfer, and a very creative cook but her hillside garden is a showplace that reflects the seasons with unusual plantings. Archie and I love having Lisa in our family. He has many Korean students, and Lisa has helped us to understand and appreciate the special nature of the Korean culture and language.

David, Chase, and I were born the first week of March and over the years we three and Doris, Archie and Lisa have helped us celebrate our birthdays. Sometimes our siblings from Syracuse join us when they are visiting California.

At holiday time each year I always remember the Christmas when my parents decided to teach little seven-year-old David a lesson for misbehaving. Instead of filling David's stocking as they had for the rest of us with an orange, some candy, and a small box of carmel corn, they filled his stocking with large chunks of coal. I will never forget the tears of disappointment on David's face. I thought my parents had another stocking ready to give to him with all the good things in it, but they did not. Ronnie began giving him some of the candy from his stocking and we all joined in. This may have been the beginning of our feeling we had to help each other, sticking together as we have throughout our lives.

Recently, David thanked me for helping him get into college. He appreciated my determination and encouragement of all my sisters and brothers to get a higher education. When I performed with choral groups in the San Francisco Bay Area, David would often come to the concerts. I loved seeing his face in the audience. Afterward, we'd compare performances and he would remind me of the times we sang together in our college choir.

David decided retirement was not challenging enough and he took a part-time position with another pharmaceutical company. He has thrown himself into learning everything possible about the medications he presents when he meets with physicians.

Not long after they were married, David and Lisa traveled to Korea so he could experience the culture first hand. They then took a trip to Italy to do the same and to meet our relatives.

$\mathcal{R}$ONALD

Ron still remembers how it felt to tug on the leg of the man who dragged our mother into the ambulance. A neighbor, Rose, grabbed and hugged six-year-old Ronnie to protect him from the violence of that moment. He still remembers the smell of the flour on Rose's apron as she held him close to her. He told me that the trauma of not being able to protect our mother kept him from visiting the state hospital when he became an adult and he still regrets his inability to visit her.

Following his years in the Air Force, Ronald found his life work in the food industry in Syracuse, first as a food broker, then as Vice President of Retail Merchandise. He had always longed to own a restaurant and finally realized his dream. With his wife Sharon and their daughter Dorie Lyn, they became chefs and co-owners of a popular Italian restaurant, which they ran for fifteen years. Ron is also proud of their son, John, who recently retired from the Air Force after twenty-two years and lives in Utah. John and his wife, Edith, have two daughters, Michaela and Alison, and one grandaughter, Isabella. Grandfather Ron, is devoted to Dorie's only child, Logan, who is in high school in Syracuse and plays guitar in a band.

Ron has always been a generous person. We all remember when he first came home after his discharge from the Air Force with white wool blazers for each of his four sisters. None of us had ever had such expensive jackets, and we were delighted. Ron always brought us gifts--one time a set of silverware, and glassware—and always coolers filled with food. Every time Ron arrived with a load of food I thought of our Sicilian relatives sending my father and me on our way with a carful of goodies. Ron and Sharon have taken in our father, Chase, and Charlotte when they needed a place to stay.

During my frequent phone conversations with Ron, I have been surprised to hear how deeply the early trauma still affects him. But despite the past, I am happy to see that he has carved out a successful life in his careers and as a devoted father and grandfather.

$\mathcal{D}$ORIS

At seventeen when Doris graduated from high school she left Elmcrest and lived with Rosalie and her husband for nearly a year. Doris chose a career in the airline industry and during her twenty years with them, she enjoyed exploring the world. Despite her erratic schedule, she attended college, then moved to California where she worked in sales with the Oakland Athletics baseball organization and with the Oakland Raiders. She enjoys showing off one of her prized possessions--the ring awarded to all the employees of the Oakland A's team when they won the World Series. I enjoy watching people seek her out at an Oakland A's game. People seem to intuit when she is in the stadium and she sometimes receives the same kind of attention as the ballplayers.

Recently, Doris launched a new career in real estate, and has become a successful realtor in Palo Alto. Though she never married, Doris has many friends who have become a kind of second family, some of whom we have included in our Messina family gatherings. Because of her outgoing personality and her positive attitude she is the one who brings people together, the party planner in our family.

Doris and I have a close relationship, and recently grew closer as we coordinated medical care for Chase during the last four months of his life. Our deep connection helped us make the right decisions during that difficult time. Doris and I especially appreciated Charlotte's visit to California when she tended Chase, giving Doris and me the respite we needed. When Chase was depressed during his last days, he always looked forward to a visit from Doris, who had the ability to pull him out of his depression, seeing the positive side of his many dilemmas. She could make him laugh when no one else could. I remember a scene when Chase was telling the young dietician what he would and would not eat. Doris arrived just at the time to remind Chase that he did not want cottage cheese. "Yes," he said, "that's right, NO COTTAGE CHEESE, got it? NO COTTAGE CHEESE!" And then he laughed, "Lots of chocolate ice cream and NO COTTAGE CHEESE!" Doris, Chase and I laughed as the dietician nodded and took down his requests.

Each time Doris visited us in London, her smiling face and openness endeared her to our friends, who have in turn embraced her as a friend. She is always so much fun to be with, because she has such a positive outlook and sees the good in people. Even when she was faced with the diagnosis of breast cancer, she conveyed such a confident attitude that all of her family and friends have taken on her positive and courageous outlook. Bouncy, upbeat, and with a great sense of humor Doris brings out the best in others.

CHARLOTTE

After divorcing her first husband, Charlotte returned to Syracuse with her daughter Susan and lived with Ron and Sharon until she married Gordon, a chemist, who had four children and lived in her neighborhood. Together, they had a son and raised their six children as a close-knit family: Michael, Christine, Scott, Michele, Susan, and Douglas. Now they have six grandchildren, and enjoy attending their sports events, often traveling many miles on a weekend to support and cheer them on.

For over thirty years, Charlotte had many interesting jobs supervising Information Technology: in a bank, a Fortune 500 company, and the Upstate Medical University in Syracuse. Charlotte is a volunteer: for the Red Cross, and more recently for fund raising events for breast cancer research. Since retirement, Charlotte and Gordon are avid golfers, often rising before six in the morning to play nine holes. She is an active elder in her presbyterian church, where she faithfully participates in many activities: cooking for potlucks, selling pies at holiday times, baking cookies for exchanges, she is active in Bible study, and frequently is the liturgist for Sunday services.

Charlotte and I were both diagnosed with breast cancer about the same time. This brought us closer together since we frequently compared our experiences of surgery and treatment. Although we live three thousand miles apart, I feel very close to Charlotte, often communicating with her several times a day by email or by phone. While traveling to Italy, Charlotte and Gordon spent a day with cousin Dino and some of our other cousins. I was thrilled that another one of my sisters had the opportunity to connect with our Italian relatives. They were impressed that Charlotte had taken an Italian language class so that she could talk with them. Now Charlotte and I have even more to talk about.

She, too, came to visit Archie and me in London, and I enjoyed showing her the city and introducing her to our friends. I'm proud of the way Charlotte has grown to become the person I always thought she was meant to be: wife, mother, grandmother, and an active member of her church and community.

FRANCIS (CHASE)

Francis never liked his name. As a child he was often teased with "Isn't that a girl's name?" When he became an adult, he changed his name to Chase. He was married briefly in his twenties and worked as a chef in Hawaii, in Mexico, and Europe. For long periods, sometimes as long as two years, no one in the family heard from him, but eventually he would turn up and tell us unbelievable stories of his escapades. Although he had not completed high school, he told us he had taught psychology in a southern California university. Another time he told us he had worked on a ship that took him to the Phillipines.

When he was in Mexico, he became ill with hepatitis, and an older American woman, Patricia, who lived in Puerto Vallarta, nursed him back to health. He remained devoted to her for saving his life. When they moved back to San Francisco, he lived with her from time to time in the Haight-Ashbury district. When they had disagreements he would leave for a few weeks or months, only to return to her open arms, and all would be forgiven. One of the ways he charmed Patricia was by bringing a special treat for her dog.

In 1984, during Archie's first sabbatical in London, Chase came to visit us at the same time our cousin Dino arrived from

Tuscany. Chase insisted on taking the four of us to the Savoy Hotel for a special dinner. Knowing the Savoy was expensive, I asked him if he had enough money for the four of us and reminded him that Archie and I were on a very limited budget, and that we could not afford the Savoy. He insisted that he did. We four dressed in our best clothes and took the Underground to the Savoy. We enjoyed our meals and when the check arrived, Chase admitted he did not have enough money. Dino began hunting for a credit card. Of course, we did not want him to pay. Archie used his credit card and we both knew that our grocery money would be very limited for the next month. I was furious with Chase. He never apologized.

When Archie and I returned home to California, Chase decided to stay in London, and found a job working in one of the many schools catering to European students who came to London to learn English. The Bell family who were running such a school hired Chase to cook and supervise the students who helped with meal preparation. Mr. Bell, a solicitor, asked Chase to assist him with a legal case that involved an American client. Chase went to court with Mr. Bell, who had asked him to speak before the judge. From then on, Chase bragged that he had been an attorney and practiced law in London — an example of how he could embellish reality.

As his time ran out in London, Chase bought an old van and drove to the continent. He arrived at Dino's home in Tuscany where he collapsed just as the van broke down. Dino could see that Chase was ill, and generously arranged for him to see a doctor. Dino's wife, Grace, had died of leukemia when their three children were quite young. He worked in a bank and, with a little help from his mother, was raising his children alone. He certainly did not need Chase to add to his burdens, but he recognized that Chase had nowhere to turn for medical care and was too sick to leave. Dino and his children took care of Chase for three months until he was well enough to return to the States. Years later, I learned of Chase's dependence on Dino and his family, and I was ashamed of Chase's imposition on our cousin.

Chase's problems were not over. In 1987 while waiting to cross the street in downtown San Francisco, he was struck by a bus that had jumped the curb. He remained in a coma for three days, suffering brain trauma. Then other medical problems developed. He lost the sight in one eye from a stroke, and had heart and lung problems. Unable to work, he lived on a ranch north of San Francisco. Fortunately, since he was a veteran, he was able to receive his medical care from the Veterans Administration.

In 2002 he was diagnosed with cardiomyopathy and told he might have six months to live. He defied the diagnosis and during the next four years he traveled to Alaska and Hawaii and was proud to outlive the prognosis. However, as his health began to decline Doris and I tried to manage his medical care, but Chase was strong-willed and sometimes overruled the plans we made. At one point he abruptly terminated hospice, causing Doris and me to increase our travel back and forth to Santa Rosa to tend to his needs. When his friends recognized his decline, they organized a "celebration of life" party. Over one hundred of his friends came from near and far to honor him. Chase was moved to tears by their love for him.

When Chase finally agreed he needed twenty-four hour care, he was admitted to the palliative care unit of the Veterans Medical Center in San Francisco where Doris and I continued to visit him almost every day as we had during the previous four months. David played an important role in clearing the clutter Chase had accumulated throughout his life as Doris and I managed and monitored his day-to-day decline.

Before he died of congestive heart failure in 2006, Chase had arranged to donate his body to the University of California at San Francisco for scientific research and education. A bench with a plaque dedicated to him overlooks Onondaga Lake in Syracuse, a favorite park we all enjoyed as children.

Chase was an enigma. Probably no one knew everything about him for he moved in and out of people's lives with his bizarre stories about where he had been and what he had done. All his sisters and brothers welcomed him warmly but with some reserve, not knowing how much to trust him. I would be angry with him and then he would turn on the charm and all would be forgotten, if not always forgiven. Others in our family had a similar relationship with Chase. We loved him, he was our brother, but we all had stories to tell of how he had taken advantage us in various ways.

$\mathcal{V}$INCENT

Our youngest brother, Vincent has lived in Syracuse all his life. He has three children from his first marriage: Amber, Carol, and Nathan. Vincent has always impressed me with his devotion as a father. When the children were very young he prepared their meals, read to then each night, and enjoyed nurturing them. He had learned how to take care of infants in the foster home where he had grown up.

He has worked for the same company in Syracuse for almost thirty years where he wrote software and provided technical and software support to many libraries across the country. For the last ten years he has been in sales, visiting the libraries and attending conferences where many of the librarians have become personal friends.

When Vince talks about his growing-up years, he expresses gratitude to the Van Marter family he lived with for the first nineteen years of his life, a stable foster home in the rural outskirts of Syracuse. He believes he avoided many of the problems our other brothers had at Elmcrest, especially the abuse.

As a young man, Vince enjoyed athletics, especially "running so fast you almost feel to be in flight," as he put it. He remembers fondly the major league baseball game in Cleveland he attended when he came to visit as a teenager. He says a highlight of his childhood was that Indians and Yankees game. His wife, Elizabeth, is a librarian in a small town near Syracuse. Libbie and Vince are avid gardeners and golfers. During the summer he worked part-time at the shop at a golf course sometimes with the help of his three children. For years most of us did not stay in touch with Vince's three children, Amber, Carol, and Nathan. Since he has been married to Libbie we have enjoyed getting to know them.

Although Vincent did not have the Elmcrest experiences, he had his own foster home experience, which was a positive one for him. As an adult he has been embraced by all his brothers and sisters. He feels he has two families: the one that raised him, the Van Merters, and the one he was born into, the Messinas.

I enjoy keeping in touch with Vincent via email because he has a delightful sense of humor. I wish we lived closer so we could visit in person more often. After so many years of missing Vincent, we all are proud to finally have him a full member of our family.

$\mathcal{D}$ADDY

Dad had spent his last five years realizing his dream of living in Sicily during the winter months and in upstate New York each summer. After my first trip to Italy, I saw my father every summer when he returned to the states. I met his plane in Boston, and he would spend a few days with Archie and me in Worcester before traveling to Victor, NY to spend the rest of the summer at Rosalie's home. We smile when we remember that we never could get him to say "Victor." It was always "Victory."

We like to remind each other of the early years when our father took us to the lots where he planted tomatoes, peppers, and zucchini, tended the beehive, and proudly brought home pears, peaches, cherries, and grapes each autumn. When the lots were no longer available to him, he planted tomatoes on the small plot behind our house. I still think of him as having a love of farming and making us the best soup and pasta. Although we complained about not having enough variety in our meals, we loved his soup and pasta.

Our father, Frank, (Francisco) died in September of 1968 at the age of seventy-five, in a hospital in upstate New York following prostate surgery. Archie officiated at our Dad's funeral service where our brothers, sisters, a cousin, and Aunt Fay were present. (Chase was not present and no one heard from him for another two years.)

When my siblings and I are together, we enjoy telling amusing stories of our father. One of our favorites:

Once Dad was disappointed with the shoddy work of city employees who were to fix a pothole in the street at the end of our driveway. When the workers were on their lunch break, Dad took their equipment, made a much larger hole, filled it with gravel, and was about to add the tar when the workers discovered what he had done. They called the police and after much wrangling, Dad was able to convince the police that the city workers had done a poor job. He explained how the hole would appear every year after severe winter weather. He said he knew how to fix the hole once and for all. Fortunately, the police did not arrest him. Dad was right. He had done an excellent job of patching the hole and it never opened up again.

We have all made peace with our father and his imprisonment, though we never talk about those difficult years. We have forgiven him.

𝓜OM

Our mother, Almerinda, lived in institutions for fifty-four years. Forty-eight of those years were spent in Marcy State hospital near Rome, New York. Her last years were in a comfortable and caring catholic nursing home in Utica, New York. We were surprised to learn that none of the staff of the nursing home knew she'd had a lobotomy when she was thirty-six years old. The staff told us that every day she repeated the names of her children; perhaps it was her way of never forgetting us. They told us she had a sweet disposition, loved to sing, sometimes in Italian, and often led the residents in Christmas carols. In 2002, at the age of eighty-nine, Mother died of colon cancer. Together, Archie and Rosalie co-officiated at her funeral, despite the fact that Rosalie was in a wheelchair. We all shared what we remembered about our mother. Most of us have few memories of our mother, since she was taken from us at such an early age. Rosalie and I especially enjoyed her love of reading, music and her faith. When Rosalie sang Mom's favorite hymns, she would be reminded of her beautiful voice, singing while preparing meals for our family.

Chase said he had no recollection of her before his fourteenth birthday, but he always remembered her sweet temperament when he visited her in the state hospital. David remembered how he had shared Mom's love of jigsaw puzzles.

On one occasion she was allowed to leave the State Hospital for one of our family reunions. She spent most of the time engrossed in a jigsaw puzzle. We each took turns working on the puzzle with her. She seemed very distant and unable to engage any of us, but became very animated when she began to eat the delicious Italian food that Ron, Sharon and Dorie had prepared for us all.

Ron was never able to visit Mom at the hospital but his daughter Dorie did visit her grandmother a number of times. I saw my Mother almost every time I traveled to Syracuse. I always remembered Aunt Fay's suggestion to send her cards and notes for holidays, especially on Mothers' Day. I know my mother treasured them when I visited I saw they were displayed on her dresser. Charlotte and Vincent, who kept the closest contact with Mom during her last years, had no memories of her as a "well" woman, since they both were so young when she was taken to the state hospital, but they were the most faithful of all of us, visiting her regularly and monitoring her care. I was touched when I learned that Libbie, Vincent's wife, would also visit my mother, even without Vincent.

A friend of the family spoke at Mom's funeral about how impressed she was at the strength of character we each had developed in spite of our difficult circumstances growing up. She commended us for "sticking together."

*A*UNT FAY

Fay Zampi Palma, my mother's sister, was special to all of us. We felt close to her and admired her care of our family. Aunt Fay had supported our grandmother, giving her daily insulin shots Grandma wouldn't give herself. Aunt Fay took care of Grandma until she died in her eighties. At that time I was still in college and regretted that I was unable to attend Grandma's funeral.

When Aunt Fay was fifty years old, she surprised all of us by marrying her minister after he had become a widower. Some of his children had difficulty accepting Aunt Fay, though she assured them she was not trying to take their mother's place. She was only interested in taking care of their father in his advanced years. The happiest years of her life were the four years when she was married to Michael Palma. For two of those years, she nursed him after he had a stroke. By the time of his death, his children had come to appreciate how Fay had cared for their father and they treated her more kindly. Aunt Fay showed us how a family nurtures each other.

I looked forward to the letters of encouragement Aunt Fay sent me every month or so during my college and seminary years. Occasionally she would send me a little money. She always inquired about what books I read and what I was learning. I told her about Howard Thurman's books, and sent her one I knew she would enjoy. Aunt Fay is the only one who regularly kept in touch with me and my spiritual development. She regretted never having gone to college or seminary, through me she could vicariously experience it.

Archie and I were delighted when she agreed to visit us after she retired from her position as Secretary to the Dean at Onondaga Community College. We had a wonderful time showing her the Bay Area, and she especially loved Monterey Bay. She enjoyed walking along the beach, learning about the sea birds, and marveling at the quality of the fruits and vegetables in California.

At the time of her death in August 1991, Aunt Fay had been teaching Sunday School for over seventy years. A long-time friend of Aunt Fay's, Joanna, asked me about each of my siblings and about Archie. I was surprised that she knew our names. She told me she and Aunt Fay phoned each other every day for forty years and prayed for us, calling each of us by our names. Why should I have been surprised? Aunt Fay was our angel.

*G*iven our backgrounds, my siblings and I could easily have become criminal justice or mental illness statistics like our parents, but we all were determined to have a better life and to pursue our dreams as healthy, law-abiding citizens. Through music and my spiritual life, I had a vision that education would be the key ingredient for improving our lives.

Beginning with the Elmcrest staff, we found supportive, caring people—Aunt Fay, ministers, teachers, friends, and therapists who provided the parenting we needed to grow and develop into healthy adults.

During our childhood, we had to deny our pain about losing our mother. Aware of society's attitudes towards mental illness and imprisonment, it seemed easier to pretend that our parents were dead. Elmcrest had provided us a safe home and our partners offered most of us the companionship and love we desired and deserved.

Some of us have found our faith in God to be a sustaining comfort throughout our lives. I think of my faith as my "saving grace." I cannot imagine living without continual dependence on prayer, meditation, and music to sustain, guide me, and give me inner strength.

I have come to appreciate more than ever my father's wisdom in insisting that the social worker find a place like the orphanage where we could all be together, instead of splitting us up and sending us to separate foster homes. When we grew too old for Elmcrest, I did my best to hold our famly together. Archie, my devoted husband and friend, deserves a lot of credit for helping to create a hospitable place for my brothers, sisters, nieces, and nephews when they needed a safe haven. He has helped to make our home inviting for family gatherings, especially during holidays.

A memoir can be healing for the writer but may also open wounds for others. My hope is that through reading the history of our family, as I see it, readers will explore their own healing for themselves and their families.

Although there were many times when I wanted to be relieved of my parenting role, I understood how important it was to feel we were still a family, and I helped to make that happen. Now when we gather, I am pleased that we all genuinely like each other and get along. I understand the part I played in keep us connected, and am glad for it. My siblings and I have helped each other financially and emotionally when it was needed and, to this day, we celebrate each other's accomplishments and joys, from new children and grandchildren to new jobs and homes.

Geraldine M. Smith

That's what a family is: the people who know you, love you despite your faults, and take care of you when you need them without demanding anything in return. I am happy and grateful to be able to say "That's our Messina family."

AFTERWORD

*E*lectro shock therapy has continued to be a treatment in some parts of the country especially for some depressed patients although after sixty years it has been refined. Patients are given sedatives before they are "shocked" and the strength of electrical currents are far less than when it was first introduced. They are sometimes given in an 'outpatient' setting. Some patients report they are helped by these treatments which allows them to lead a fairly normal life.

In the mid to late nineteen forties, Walter Freeman was the neurologist in the US who convinced state mental hospitals across the country to use the lobotomy to 'cure' mental illness. He was not a psychiatrist nor a neurosurgeon but he was a good salesman! He traveled the United States from New England to California doing as many as fifteen to twenty lobotomies in a day at the invitation of state hospitals. He taught other physicians how to sever the frontal lobe of the brain by accessing it through the eye. He was proud to tell people that he had done 2900 lobotomies until he did the last one in 1967 in Berkeley, California. By the time of his death in 1971 the lobotomy had long since been out of favor as a treatment method due to the introduction of drugs in the nineteen fifties and the questionable outcome of the lobotomy "cure."

The New York State legislature recognized the harm that had been done to so many patients by lobotomizing them. It passed legislation that those who had received lobotomies between 1948 and 1951 would be supported financially by the state of New York for the rest of their lives. Until her death in 2002 our mother's care was paid for by the state since her lobotomy was performed within that three year period. She had been hospitalized for fifty-eight years.